1974

the
concerto

The Brown Music Horizons Series

Books now available

MUSIC IN THE UNITED STATES—*Arthur C. Edwards and W. Thomas Marrocco,* U.C.L.A.

MUSIC THROUGH THE RENAISSANCE—*James C. Thomson,* University of Kansas

THE CONCERTO—*Wendell Nelson,* University of California

MUSIC OF THE ROMANTIC PERIOD—*Johannes Riedel,* University of Minnesota

MUSIC OF THE CLASSIC PERIOD—*Theodore E. Heger,* University of Michigan

The tremendous growth and interest in basic music appreciation and literature courses and the increasing emphasis on music for the general college student demands fresh approaches to teaching and learning at the introductory level.

The Music Horizons Series represents a significant attempt to meet these needs by providing students with stimulating material of high quality by an authority in the field as well as providing instructors with the advantage of complete flexibility in organizing and teaching their course. Although the individual titles are self-contained, collectively they cover the full scope of music appreciation, literature and history.

the concerto

Wendell Nelson

University of California

WM. C. BROWN COMPANY PUBLISHERS, *Dubuque, Iowa*

MUSIC SERIES

Consulting Editor
Frederick W. Westphal
Sacramento State College

Copyright © 1969 by
Wm. C. Brown Company Publishers

Library of Congress Catalog Card Number: 69-12428

Printed in the United States of America

preface

It is my purpose in this text to acquaint the general listener with one of the great instrumental forms in music history—the concerto. I am assuming the reader has some general musical knowledge but has not pursued this exciting form in depth. The approach is an analytical, though not highly technical, one dealing with selected masterworks from the Baroque, Classic, Romantic, and Contemporary periods. If I have included more piano concertos than other kinds of concertos, it is because of the enormous appeal and popularity of the piano concerto. At least two major composers, Mozart and Beethoven, wrote more concertos for piano than for any other solo instrument.

At the ends of chapters I have listed readily accessible materials for additional reading as well as suggested listening. These lists are carefully selected though not intended to be exhaustive.

I am indebted, first of all, to my wife, Marjorie, whose many suggestions have been incorporated in this text. Without her patient assistance the writing of this book would have been impossible. I wish to thank Miss Elizabeth Heimerl for her careful typing of the manuscript. I am indebted to my colleagues, Dr. John Gillespie and Dr. Roger Nyquist, for their kindness in reading the manuscript. I am also indebted to my many classes in music history and literature. They have been inspiring laboratories in my attempt to sharpen the perception and understanding of great music.

Wendell Nelson

contents

the concerto idea

Among all the various types of instrumental compositions in music literature, probably none evokes as much excitement on the part of performer and listener alike as the concerto. The very word itself conjures up visions of musical prowess and technical virtuosity which are required in abundance if the concerto performer is to project his instrument over the massive sound of the orchestra. As opera is the fulfillment of many a singer's dream so the concerto is the *tour de force* of the instrumentalist. He becomes the star and the center of attention; indeed, he occupies a role not unlike that of the opera *prima donna*.

The concerto, as it is known today, implies a musical work of considerable prominence. It may be a work of great importance, and perhaps even a monumental composition. Beginning with the last part of the eighteenth century, the concerto has belonged principally to the piano. The piano is unique among solo instruments in its dynamic capabilities, making it an ideal "opponent" for even the largest orchestra, and composers from Mozart to Samuel Barber have written many of their most significant compositions for piano and orchestra. There are, of course, many excellent concertos for violin and other orchestral instruments, but the concerto literature for these instruments is neither as rich nor as prolific as that for the piano.

To trace the origin of the concerto it is necessary to go back in time a number of centuries, for the concerto evolved from rather modest beginnings and, after a period of several hundred years, finally emerged in its present form. The term "concerto" has been used to describe a wide variety of musical compositions, from sixteenth-century madrigals to contemporary twentieth-century concertos. While the theoretical meaning of the word has not always remained the same from century to century, its general connotation—that of two or more voices or instruments performing together, or more specifically, performing in contrasting groups—has continued unchanged.

Although the solo concerto dates back only some two and a half centuries, its foundations may be found in the most elemental sources of music. Whenever one or two people, or even as many as a small ensemble, appear in musical competition, as it were, with the larger or principal group, the concerto idea is present. It is easy to recognize this concerto idea in the modern solo concerto, but perhaps a little more difficult to visualize this same principle in anything as remote as sixteenth-century church music for antiphonal choirs. But it is these compositions, far removed from contemporary ears and from the present-day concept of the term "concerto," that contain the origin of the concerto idea.

One of the most important musical centers in sixteenth-century Europe was Venice. At that time, a powerful city in its own right, Venice ranked second only to Rome as a place of distinction among Italian cities. Musical life in Venice centered around the great Cathedral of St. Mark to which many of the finest musicians of Italy were attracted. Only music of the highest quality could meet the exacting requirements of both the Church and the Venetian State, so the positions for choirmaster and organist at the Cathedral were coveted posts, and both the competition and the examinations for these positions were rigid. As a result, there gathered at the Cathedral of St. Mark men who were not only fine performers or conductors, but high-ranking composers as well. During the sixteenth century the great Netherlands-born composer Adrian Willaert, Donati, Merulo, Andrea Gabrieli, and the greatest of the Venetian masters, Giovanni Gabrieli, held posts at the Cathedral of St. Mark.

Inside the Cathedral were two organs, placed on opposite sides of the church. Making full use of this resource, together with a choir performing with each of the organs, the Venetian composers developed music using the concerto idea, or music which contained competing or contrasting groups. Willaert was among the first to use this type of performance in his music for antiphonal choirs, a style which was particularly suited to the architecture of the Cathedral. These poly-choral compositions introduced the spatial element, the contrast between voices and instruments, and the echo effects which have remained characteristic of music in the concerto style.

Giovanni Gabrieli (1557-1612) developed further the concerto idea and made significant contributions to the literature in this style. Gabrieli's music is boldly sonorous and clearly suggestive of a highly imaginative realization of both the musical and physical resources available at the great Venetian Cathedral. Gabrieli carried the concerto idea a step further than previous composers when he wrote for vocal choruses in contrast with orchestral choruses, and for choral ensembles distinguished from solo ensembles.

Figure 1. A chorus of the Baroque period, inspired by the new plan of a resurgent Church, intones in praise of God. Using more than one orchestra, Giovanni Gabrieli, a Venetian, created a new style of great emotional power and sensuous glow. Courtesy of the Bettmann Archive.

The concerto, then, began as an idea or as a method of performing. The differences between a Gabrieli antiphonal motet and a Beethoven concerto are many—differences in texture, melodic and harmonic concepts, rhythmic practice, other musical elements—but the concerto *idea* is the same.

In the great Baroque era the minds of several musical geniuses brought new shape and substance to the idea and gave it added importance among an ever enlarging number of instrumental forms.

BASIC LISTENING:

GABRIELI, GIOVANNI, *In Ecclesiis*
                   Canzoni for Brass Choirs
                   Sonata pian' e forte

ADDITIONAL READING:

BAUER, MARION and PEYSER, ETHEL, *Music Through the Ages.* Third edition edited and revised by Elizabeth E. Rogers. New York: G. P. Putnam's Sons, 1967. Chapter 10.

DAVISON, ARCHIBALD T. and APEL, WILLI, *Historical Anthology of Music,* Vol. I. Cambridge: Harvard University Press, 1949. Example 157 (p. 234).

NALLIN, WALTER E., *The Musical Idea.* New York: The Macmillan Company, 1968. Chapter 12.

the baroque concerto

During the early Baroque era, the concerto idea found expression and further refinement in music that was referred to as being in "concertato" style. When the term *concertato* first appeared, it signified not only the use of contrasted or competing groups but probably more importantly it described music in which instruments and voices were used together. This practice of employing instruments as an accompaniment for vocal music was a significant and far-reaching contribution of the early Baroque. In time, the term *a cappella* came to refer to all music performed by voices alone while music in concertato style required voices and instruments as well. Before a really distinctive instrumental style developed in concertato music, it was necessary for both time and experience to work their separate courses. In the earliest music in concertato style, the instrumental line, called *basso continuo,* was generally nothing more than a duplication of the lowest vocal part which provided stable support for the upper, vocal lines.

The emergence of the Baroque concerto was dependent upon one factor perhaps more than any other; namely, the establishment of tonality. The instrumental concerto evolved in the Baroque only when tonality had been fully established and when melody began to be dependent upon harmonic structure to a greater extent. Other factors, of course, were prominent and extremely important as well. The texture of late Baroque music underwent a change away from the older polyphonic style with basso continuo toward the more homophonic style of the approaching Classical era. The use by composers of new harmonic patterns, notably the circle-of-fifths progressions which swept the music through many keys, was a device common to the concerto style of the late Baroque and made possible only by reason of the newly-established tonality. The harmonic structure, having gained considerably in importance, in turn exerted its newly-found influence upon the melody which was employed more and more often now in its role of defining the key. By the late Baroque the old polyphonic order was fading and the new homophonic style, much more compatible to the concerto and indeed necessary for the solo concerto, began to merge.

CORELLI

The concerto as a definite and distinct type of composition appeared in three different forms in the late Baroque: the orchestral concerto, a composition usually in several movements and utilizing a style which gave emphasis to the first violin and bass parts; the concerto grosso which contrasted a small solo group, usually strings but sometimes wind instruments (called *solo* or *concertino*), against the larger ensemble (called *tutti* or *ripieno*); and the solo concerto in which special prominence was afforded a single instrument, usually the violin, against the orchestra as a whole.

The earliest examples of actual Baroque concertos (as distinguished from compositions which display only concerto principles) are the twelve concerti grossi of Arcangelo Corelli (1653-1713). Corelli was working not only with a new style but also with the new resource of tonality in these compositions, so it is not surprising to find that his concertos are patterned after the familiar and traditional *sonata da chiesa* (church sonata) and *sonata da camera* (chamber sonata)—forms in which the composer felt completely at home. All of Corelli's concerti grossi are cast in the molds of these earlier forms. Many contain five or or more movements; many of the movements are in contrapuntal style and there are also many dance movements.

Corelli divided his concerto orchestra into two groups: the tutti, or ripieno, and the solo group, or concertino. Each group had its own continuo. For his concertino, Corelli used a string trio consisting of two violins and continuo. The string trio was a popular form of seventeenth-century chamber music and was easily and logically assimilated into the concerto grosso. There was no musical distinction or differentiation in style between the solo and the tutti in the Corelli concertos. The two groups were usually used for echo effects or to provide loud and soft dynamic contrasts. Nor did Corelli use any consistent organization of material in his concertos such as appear in later works of the period. He did make use, though, of highly idiomatic writing for the violin, and in the twelfth and last of the concerti grossi he emphasized the first violin part of the concertino, a giant step in the direction of the later solo violin concerto.

TORELLI

Toward the end of the seventeenth century new achievements in the development of the concerto were realized by another Italian composer, Giuseppe Torelli (d. 1708). Although Torelli composed his first concerti grossi in the manner of the church and chamber sonatas and along the same general lines as Corelli, he then deviated from these types and composed concertos for orchestra, works in concerto style but not dependent on the characteristic of two contrasted groups or sections. Instead, Torelli emphasized melodic qualities in both the first violin and the bass parts.

Torelli standardized, by consistent usage, the three-movement work (fast-slow-fast) which later composers were to use almost entirely. In form, Torelli made significant contributions, most notably in the *allegro* movements where the exposition of the themes and the use of key relationships were accomplishments of considerable importance. His concerto techniques became nearly synonymous with the style itself: the driving rhythms, the use of triadic themes which quickly define the key at the onset of the movement, and the practice of the *ritornello* form or the frequent return of the tutti.

In addition to his orchestral concertos, Torelli pioneered in the field of the solo violin concerto.* In Torelli's works the solo became of equal importance with the orchestra and in them the solo and tutti show the beginning of thematic independence. Although other composers also wrote solo violin concertos around this time or even before, Torelli is generally given credit for inaugurating the form. The solo concerto continued to increase in popularity and in stature during the late Baroque and on into subsequent periods.

VIVALDI

One of the most important of the Baroque concerto writers and one who left an indelible imprint on the style was Antonio Vivaldi (c. 1676-1741). A prolific composer, Vivaldi wrote concertos almost to the exclusion of other types of instrumental music, though much of his work

---

*The forerunners of the solo concerto were the orchestral concertos or the concerti grossi which featured a brilliant passage in the violin part. From these it was a logical step to a composition for alternating solo and tutti.

still remains unpublished. Even so, there are today about 450 extant
Vivaldi concertos.

Vivaldi was another of the great Italian composers whose musical
life was centered in Venice. As conductor, composer, teacher, and general
superintendent of music at the conservatory of the Pietá, it was Vivaldi's
function to provide new concertos and other required music for each
festival. The fact that the festivals were numerous and Vivaldi's students
highly competent must have contributed in no small measure to the
composer's tremendous output.

Vivaldi's concerti grossi follow the same general form as those of
Torelli. Most of Vivaldi's concertos are in the three-movement scheme,
though he does not use this plan exclusively, and he employs the ritornello technique which Torelli initiated, enlarging it significantly and
even allowing the ritornello to appear in other keys during the movement. There is less contrapuntal writing in Vivaldi's concertos than in
those of the earlier Baroque composers. Vivaldi's texture is usually homophonic with extremely vital rhythmic drive. His melodies are fresh and
captivating; they often follow the earlier Baroque custom of initially
outlining the key. The harmonic structure is definite and is vigorously
defined by Vivaldi's abundant use of sequential patterns.

Vivaldi was particularly skillful in his treatment of solo and tutti
sections, and in the Vivaldi concertos the soloist occupies a dominant
and dramatic position against the orchestra as a whole. Rather than
give the soloist mere decorative material or ornamentation of a virtuosic
nature, unrelated to the orchestral subject matter, Vivaldi permits his
soloists to expand and embellish the themes presented in the tutti. In
a few isolated instances he goes so far as to give the soloist new subject
matter of his own, but this technique was not to become common practice until the Classic period to follow.

Vivaldi's orchestra usually included strings with either organ or
harpsichord continuo, though in some concertos he achieved expressive
and quite remarkable tone coloring by the use of wind instruments as
well. The concertino in the Vivaldi concertos was treated in a more
independent fashion than had been the previous custom. Vivaldi expanded or reduced the number of players to suit the purpose at hand,
and even in the solo concertos there is often more than one instrument
in the concertino parts.

Vivaldi was fond of using programmatic titles for his concertos, the
most famous probably being *Le Stagioni* (The Seasons), in which each
of the four movements of the concerto represents a different season
of the year. Though Vivaldi indulged in descriptive writing such as the

imitations of bird calls and running water, he allowed himself such freedom only in the solo sections. In the remainder of the music he maintained a strict ritornello form. *The Seasons* illustrates another contribution which Vivaldi made to the general concerto plan: he attached as much importance to the slow movements as he did to the fast and sprightly ones. Vivaldi's slow movements follow no set plan or organization of material, but they are usually characterized by a *cantabile* melody and are often in minor keys.

HANDEL

Among all of the orchestral compositions of George Frideric Handel (1685-1759), the concertos number among his most significant works. Bukofzer states that "Handel raised the Italian concerto grosso to the highest level of baroque entertainment."[1] Handel was not experimental as far as the concerto style was concerned. He seemed to prefer the older pattern of the concerto, modeled after the church and chamber sonata such as Corelli used, rather than the three-movement scheme of Vivaldi. Handel's concertos, consequently, contain from one to six movements and these range in style from solemn French overtures to elegant and courtly dances and from operatic arias to energetic double fugues. Completely at home in the Italian style of composition, Handel added to the Corelli models his own highly developed dramatic sense and his unique touch of animated genius. Handel's concerti grossi are contained mainly in two sets: Op. 3, consisting of six orchestral concertos for winds and strings, and Op. 6, a group of twelve concertos for strings alone. He also wrote concertos for individual instruments but these are in the minority.

The one type of concerto of which Handel may be called the originator is the solo concerto for organ and orchestra. The organ intended for use in these pieces is not the large pipe organ most commonly associated with Baroque organ literature but rather a small instrument with no pedal board. Handel's organ concertos, Op. 4 and Op. 7, plus a number of other concertos with no opus numbers, are light and improvisational in style, and the absence of strict contrapuntal writing marks them as being in definite contrast to his concerti grossi.

J. S. BACH

The summation of Baroque music in all styles and in all its many facets, with the exception of the opera, may be found in the works of

Johann Sebastian Bach (1685-1750), and the concerto grosso reached
the peak of its development in the hands of this master. The six Brandenburg Concertos, dating from Bach's employment at Cöthen when he
wrote mainly chamber and orchestral music, are, as Bukofzer again
reminds, "the most inspired and complex concerti grossi of the baroque
era."[2] In these works Bach combined and synthesized his own German
musical heritage and its tradition of rich, contrapuntal texture with the
Italian concerto in the Vivaldi style.

The Brandenburg Concertos are principally concerti grossi, com-
bining parts for orchestra and concertino. In the Third and Sixth Concertos Bach deviates from this style to write for orchestra alone, scoring
these works for strings and continuo only. The Fourth Brandenburg
Concerto in G major takes on the character of a solo violin concerto
with extended virtuosic writing for the principal violin. Further expanding the concerto grosso principle, Bach scores the Fifth Brandenburg
Concerto in D major for a concertino of flutes and violin, a tutti consisting of the usual strings, and a *cembalo concertato*. The harpsichord
is raised from the status of the continuo part to that of principal soloist,
and the work becomes, in effect, the first keyboard concerto.

Brandenburg Concerto No. 2 in F Major

A typical example of these great masterpieces of Baroque concerto
writing is the Second Brandenburg Concerto in F major. Requiring an
orchestra of the usual strings and continuo with a concertino consisting
of a trumpet, flute, oboe, and violin, this concerto is in the three-
movement pattern of *allegro, andante,* and *allegro assai.* The first movement, sectional in construction, contains a final return or recapitulation
of the original thematic material. Bach draws upon two principal motives
for his subject matter in this movement; the first is found in measure 1
in the violins of the tutti:

Example 1. Bach, Brandenburg Concerto No. 2, First Movement.

the second in measure 8 in the solo violin part of the concertino:

Example 2. Bach, Brandenburg Concerto No. 2, First Movement.

The second movement is scored only for flute, oboe, violin, cello, and continuo, and Bach again makes use of the canonic treatment of a lyric melody:

Example 3. Bach, Brandenburg Concerto No. 2, Second Movement.

The final movement may be divided into three main sections but there is only one theme throughout the entire movement.

Example 4. Bach, Brandenburg Concerto No. 2, Third Movement.

Prominent in this *allegro assai* is the penetrating tone of the high trumpet, an instrument which has come to be known as the "Bach trumpet." It was in common usage in Bach's time but did not survive long enough to become a standard instrument in the modern symphony orchestra.

Bach's concerto style consists generally of the alternation of solo and tutti sections as the subject material is continually expanded and unfolded. The number of appearances of either solo or tutti is not fixed and there is no mandatory sense of key relationship. Bach occasionally hints at the tonic-dominant relationship in the order of themes and keys which later became the cornerstone of sonata form. In fast movements, whether they are sectionalized, A B A, or fugues, Bach always concludes the movement with a complete recapitulation of the principal material in the original key even though he may have modulated into remote tonal centers during the course of the movement. In slow movements Bach abandons both the spirit and the techniques of the fast sections. Usually written for a smaller group of instruments, these movements are cast in a profound mood which offers a decided contrast to the surrounding *allegros*.

In addition to the six Brandenburg concertos, Bach also wrote concerti grossi for two, three, and four claviers with orchestra, the Double Violin concerto, and the Triple Concerto in A minor. His concertos for solo clavier and orchestra, though among the first of their kind, are

Figure 2. A Bach solo concerto. Courtesy of The Bettmann Archive.

arrangements of other compositions, generally violin concertos. The Suite No. 2 for flute and strings, though composed in the general outlines dictated by the suite with its succession of dance forms, may nevertheless be considered a valid solo concerto for flute. The only part of the suite which carried over into the modern concerto is the rondo.

Bach's *Concerto in Italian Style* for solo harpsichord must be cited as an example of his extension of the concerto principle and style into the realm of solo literature. Bach achieves the illusion of tutti and solo in this composition by means of the dynamic contrasts of *forte* and *piano* which he has inserted into the score. The lyric, *cantabile* writing, typical of the Italian style which Bach emulates (particularly in the second movement), gave occasion to the title *Italian Concerto.*

The solo concerto, which began almost timidly earlier in the Baroque era, became more prominent as the period came to an end, and, in the Classic period, it was this form which completely captured the field. It took some time for the solo instrument to become completely independent of the concertino of which it was originally a part and to emerge alone and dominant over the orchestra as a whole. The violin was aided in this respect by many technical improvements of the instrument and by a continued exploration by composers of its idiomatic possibilities. Insofar as the capabilities for assuming the solo rule were concerned, these advances and development of technique had far-reaching effects. The pizzicato, the tremolo, double stops, and an extended range made the instrument more fitted for its solo-tutti rivalry. Violin makers such as Amati, Guarneri, and Stradivari were improving and striving to perfect the construction of the instrument itself, and their efforts exerted a great influence upon the possibilities of an expanded technique for the violin.

Baroque concertos are not concertos in the modern sense, for the modern concerto assumes a use of sonata form which was not fully developed during the Baroque. Baroque concerto movements often use many themes but these seem to grow out of one another and expand and evolve by means of various techniques as the movement progresses. In sonata form there must be a conscious preparation for something new, and inherent in sonata form is the dramatic tension occasioned by the appearance of the secondary subject first in the dominant and finally in the tonic key. The Baroque concerto, with its principle of solo-tutti competition and its possibility of both thematic and key contrast, was the bridge or the point of contact between this era and the Classic period which followed.

BASIC LISTENING:

BACH, J. S., Brandenburg Concerto No. 2 in F major

ADDITIONAL SUGGESTED LISTENING:

CORELLI, Concerto Grosso in F major, Op. 6, No. 9
TORELLI, Concerto Grosso in D major, Op. 6, No. 10
———, Concerto in D major for Trumpet and Orchestra
VIVALDI, Le Quattro Stagioni (The Four Seasons)
———, Concerto for Piccolo and Orchestra
HANDEL, Concerto Grosso in B-flat major, Op. 6, No. 7
———, Concerto in G minor for Oboe and Orchestra
———, Concerto in B-flat major for Harp and Orchestra, Op. 4, No. 6
BACH, J. S., The Brandenburg Concertos
———, The Italian Concerto
———, Concerto No. 2 in E major for Violin and Orchestra
———, Concerto No. 1 in D minor for Piano and Orchestra

ADDITIONAL READING:

BOYDEN, DAVID D., An Introduction to Music. New York: Alfred A. Knopf,
    1966. Chapter 14, pp. 212-217.
ULRICH, HOMER, Music: A Design for Listening. New York: Harcourt,
    Brace & World, Inc., 1962. Second edition. Chapter 14, pp. 217-223;
    Chapter 15, pp. 235-239.

FOOTNOTES

[1]Manfred F. Bukofzer, Music in the Baroque Era (New York: W. W. Norton
& Company, Inc., 1947), pp. 342-343.
    [2]Ibid., p. 291.

the classic concerto

THE SPIRIT OF EIGHTEENTH-CENTURY CLASSICISM

That era of music history known as the "Classic period" embodies certain ideals and principles which require understanding in order that the musical products of the period may be fully appreciated. The term "Classic" may refer to either of two elements: time or content. The term may be used to represent a particular period in history, such as the classic era of Greek and Roman antiquity, or it may refer to any era which contains a high point of excellence in cultural values and concepts. It is the latter reference which exemplifies the music of the eighteenth century.

A number of popular misconceptions have arisen in connection with the terms "Classical" and "Romantic." A common distinction is that Classicism appeals to the intellect and Romanticism appeals to the emotions. While this is partially true, such a distinction places dangerous limitations upon the connotations of the two terms. No composer, for example, realized more fully than Mozart that the important thing in music is its spiritual quality, its soul, and its poignant emotion. The best music of the Classic period is that which illustrates the balance and proportion typical of the thought of the period yet which possesses the spiritual quality that makes it universal and timeless in its emotional appeal.

The art of any age tends to exhibit characteristics that identify it as being either predominantly Classic or predominantly Romantic. Whether in art, literature, or music, Classicism contains basic principles which, if they are predominant in the mind of the artist, result in the creation of a particular type of painting, a particular kind of essay, or a particular style of musical composition. Analysis reveals that foremost among these basic principles is the element of truth and directness—a straightforward, logical approach to life. Such an approach consists of the ability to acknowledge the emotions without becoming sentimental over them. It recognizes the necessity of disciplined emotional control, for far from excluding emotions, the Classic ideal is to integrate and relate them into a broad universal experience. As such, Classicism represents an attitude primarily *intellectual* and primarily *universal*. It attempts to subordinate passion to reason and to express feelings and traits common to mankind rather than to express individual idiosyncrasies. Classicism is never interested in emotional experience for its own sake but seeks that delicate balance of intellect and emotion which results in universality.

The Classic spirit also demands that beauty must conform to a sense of order and definiteness. No particular emphasis is placed upon size, but rather symmetry and proportion are stressed. This balance of structure is further enhanced by the Classic ideal of simplicity and clarity. These qualities, considered together, constitute a general basis for the understanding of Classicism in the art of music.

It is important to remember that there is no abrupt line of separation between any two stylistic periods in music history. The Classic period, mainly the eighteenth century and early nineteenth century, is neither a total nor isolated musical entity. Much of the music written within the boundaries of the period has characteristics of both preceding and subsequent periods. The greater part of the music composed during this time, however, possesses characteristics of style which have come to be identified with musical Classicism.

In any era music may be expected to reflect the spirit of the times. The art of music in the eighteenth century was aristocratic, intended for the palaces, the chapels, and the drawing rooms of the nobility. To suit these tastes, music had to be lyric, restrained, and in good taste. There was no place for violent emotional outbursts or obvious sentimentality. Rather a straightforward, objective, and highly intellectual approach was favored—one which could project artistic feeling with proper dignity. Mozart himself confirmed this ideal in a letter in which he explained that "passions, whether violent or not, must never be expressed in such a way as to excite disgust, and even in the most terrible situations must never cease to be *music*."[1]

In the eighteenth century the foundations of musical form, on which much of the art's later structures were built, were laid. The Classical penchant for order resulted in the stabilization of sonata form in the concerto, the symphony, and the string quartet. Clarity and simplicity of texture characterized the content of these media. The homophonic style, the emphasis upon melody, and the relative harmonic simplicity were completely in keeping with the aesthetic ideals of the times.

THE ROCOCO PERIOD

The period between J. S. Bach and Joseph Haydn is one whose style is called "galant" or Rococo. The music is graceful, courtly, and euphonious. In contrast to the polyphonic Baroque tradition of J. S. Bach, it possesses a gracious, if superficial, melodic line, a comparatively simple harmonic background, and above all, an air of elegance and refinement. Composers were discovering an exciting and divergent new outlet for the products of their art: audiences which gathered in the salons and courts of the wealthy royalty and nobility. In these secular centers, the newer style seemed more appropriate than the older, contrapuntal music whose purpose had often been church-oriented. Capable of playing highly decorative and ornamental material, keyboard instruments took on new importance. Previously relegated to continuo parts, the harpsichord added interest and excitement to the simple melodic and rhythmic textures now in vogue. It was not long before a large repertoire of keyboard concertos came into existence.

Numbering among the most important composers of the period were two of the sons of J. S. Bach, Carl Philipp Emanuel (1714-1788) and Johann Christian (1735-1782). C. P. E. Bach is probably best known for his contributions in the realm of sonata form which won him the recognition and praise of both Haydn and Mozart. Also important is the role C. P. E. Bach played in the development of new literature for the increasingly popular piano. Both his innovations in the realm of sonata form and his explorations into the potentialities of the piano secure for him a leading position among the great musicians of all time.

Of the fifty-two keyboard concertos of C. P. E. Bach, none has survived to become a part of the repertoire. These concertos, though of high quality, interest today's musicians chiefly for historical reasons. C. P. E. Bach suffers from his particular place in history: a stepping-stone and a building block, however valuable, for a changing musical style. His music, inevitably, was overshadowed by that which followed.

Johann Christian Bach is of importance to the concerto not only because of his own works in that form but also because he so strongly influenced Mozart. Touring as a child prodigy, Mozart met J. C. Bach in London where the older man had established himself as a composer of great eminence. Mozart's first compositions in concerto form (the three concertos of K. 107) are, in fact, arrangements of J. C. Bach sonatas and are proof of the high esteem in which Mozart held the older master.

J. C. Bach wrote prolifically in the concerto style and most of these works are for keyboard instruments. Their formal structure is closely related to the form as Mozart later used it. Earlier concerto composers, including C. P. E. Bach, made use primarily of one theme, elaborating it in various ways, but with J. C. Bach the beginning of a definite formal organization in first movements is observed and the familiar pattern of sonata form is clearly evident. In such concertos as the Cembalo Concerto in B-flat major, Op. 13, No. 4, J. C. Bach uses the opening orchestral tutti to introduce the principal theme of the movement, but after the solo has entered and has repeated the first theme, it states, as the second subject, a new melody in the dominant key. During the development section, the solo also introduces a theme not heard previously in the exposition. J. C. Bach accurately predicted the mature Classical concerto principle in his use of sonata form and homophonic texture. However, the general plan of the construction of the concerto as a whole was not yet consolidated by J. C. Bach nor by any of the predecessors of Mozart. Though many of the concertos of J. C. Bach are in two movements, the regular three-movement scheme as well as finer subtleties of the form did not become fully established until Mozart.

HAYDN

A most prolific composer, (Franz) Joseph Haydn (1732-1809) deserves the titles "father of the symphony" and "father of the quartet" by virtue of sheer output alone. With Haydn the Classical sonata-allegro form became completely realized and served him well in his masterful creations. In addition to the symphony and string quartet, Haydn wrote piano sonatas, other chamber music, operas, and sacred music. Because his genius is not evenly distributed throughout all these works, many have not survived the time and circumstances in which they were written. This does not diminish Haydn's importance nor his tremendous contribution to music.

The realm of the concerto is one in which Haydn is not remembered most significantly. Though he composed a large number of concertos, they are generally considered to be less important than many of his other works. Concertos for violin, cello, double-bass, baryton (an instrument similar to the viola da gamba, possessing an extra set of sympathetically vibrating strings), lyre, trumpet, and some twenty keyboard concertos present a diverse collection of compositions for solo and orchestra. The Klavier Concerto in D major, with its particularly fine last movement, is perhaps the best known of the Haydn concertos and one of the few ever to be performed today.

MOZART

The concerto in the Classic period reached a peak of artistic perfection in the works of Wolfgang Amadeus Mozart (1756-1791). He took the Classic ideal and the concerto principle of opposition and contrast and made of them something expressive, dramatic, and subtle— the Classical concerto.

Mozart lived in an age dominated by Italian music, particularly the Italian opera, and to understand Mozart's compositions, whether operatic or not, it is essential to perceive the tremendous influence which the Italian opera exerted over his life and his work. Even as a child Mozart took delight in hearing music in the Italian operatic style and he turned at an early age to the writing of works in this form. His intense love for lyricism and beauty found its ideal channel of expression through the Italian operatic medium. In his letters Mozart constantly speaks of his interest in the opera. Writing to his sister in March of 1770, he says, "I cannot count exactly, but I really believe we have been six or seven times to the opera. . . ."[2] Again in December, 1772, he writes to his sister from Milan: "I cannot possibly write much, for I have no news to tell you, and furthermore I do not know what I am writing because I think of nothing but my opera (Lucio Silla), and am in danger of putting down an aria instead of words!"[3] Leopold Mozart, in a letter to his wife in December, 1770, makes an interesting commentary upon the young Mozart's facility at composing in the Italian style:

> Before the first rehearsal with the small orchestra, there were plenty of persons who made satirical remarks and cried down the music in advance as something immature and feeble—people who 'prophesied,' so to speak, affirming that it was impossible for a young boy, and a German into the bargain, to write an Italian opera; for although they recognized him as a great virtuoso, they could not believe he could have the requisite understanding of and insight into the *chiaro ed oscuro* of the stage. Since the night of the first small rehearsal, however, all these people have been struck dumb and left without a word to say.[4]

As Mozart's character and musicianship matured, his interest in the Italian opera grew until it became his greatest ambition to succeed in the writing of operas. In a letter to his father dated February 4, 1778, he says, ". . . do not forget my ambition to write operas. I am jealous of everybody who writes one. I could weep for vexation when I hear or see an aria."[5] In another letter of October, 1777, he writes, "Simply to hear any one speak of an opera, or to be in the theatre, is enough to make me beside myself."[6] And again, in 1782 he writes, "Opera to me comes before anything else."[7]

Though it was Mozart's desire to be known as an opera composer, his early fame was closely associated with his unusual facility at the keyboard. As a child prodigy he was famous throughout Europe; as a mature artist his career also depended considerably upon his piano playing. Largely to satisfy his own needs for new compositions, Mozart wrote 24 piano concertos, 5 concertos for the violin (on which he also performed), and concertos for a variety of other instruments. Mozart's concertos emulate his operas, for these instrumental compositions are consistently vocal in concept. Slow movements, in particular, suggest coloratura arias.

Mozart wrote concertos from early childhood until the very last months of his life. When he was four years old his father discovered him busily composing a concerto for clavecin and was impressed with the boy's correct observance of the rules of composition. Mozart's first concertos were for keyboard and were arrangements rather than original compositions. It may be assumed that Mozart conceived them as exercises useful in acquainting him with the procedures of concerto writing. By the age of eleven, however, Mozart had already established the general outlines of concerto form which he employed in the remainder of his compositions in this genre.

The Classic concerto poses problems for the composer which are not found in other types of compositions. By far the majority of these problems are focused in the first movement. It is here that the composer must artfully arrange the themes so that what emerges is a true Classic concerto and not a Classic symphony. That subtle relationship between solo and orchestra which must be fitted into the strict confines of the sonata-allegro form provides the difficulties, challenges, and excitement inherent in the first movement of the Classic concerto.

Basically, the design of the first movements of a concerto, symphony, or sonata of the Classic period is the same. There are three principal sections: the exposition, or the presentation of the themes, the first in the key of the tonic, the second in a related key, usually the dominant; the development section, or the working out of the previously presented material in a variety of possible ways; and the recapitulation, or the return of the initial themes with the second subject this time appearing in the key of the tonic. To this basic pattern may be added transition themes, closing themes, and coda, or ending, sections, but the fundamental requirements of the sonata form remain unchangeable.

Figure 3. The young Mozart, at about 1786, in front of a piano. Painting in the Mozarteum, Salzburg. Courtesy of The Bettmann Archive.

It is the custom in the Classic concerto for the orchestra to introduce many, or all, of the themes in the opening tutti. Here the imagination and skill of the composer are highly challenged, for the problem is to prevent the opening tutti from progressing into a regular symphony movement before the soloist has even entered. Equally challenging is the task of keeping the soloist supplied with interesting material after the orchestra has already presented the majority of the thematic substance. Mozart, whose unerring skill in matters of form has never been surpassed, deftly handled the difficulties of this double exposition in the Classic concerto from his earliest youthful concerto compositions, but Beethoven struggled a good part of his life with these problems and did not approach a resolution until his last concertos. To avoid the effort of wrestling with formal disciplines of such significance, many Romantic and contemporary composers eliminated the double exposition and even the opening tutti entirely, permitting the soloist to become immediately the dominating factor in the concerto. Mozart chose to prepare carefully the opening orchestral tutti so that the entrance of the soloist would be a dramatic moment.

Violin Concerto in D Major, K. 218

The opening of the year 1775 found Mozart in Munich for the production of his opera *La finta giardiniera*. He returned to Salzburg in time to compose *Il Re pastore* for the visit of the Archduke Maximilian in April, and he remained there the rest of the year. This was a rather prolific year in terms of the number of compositions. In addition to the two operas mentioned above, Mozart wrote several church compositions and solo arias, one piano sonata, and the five violin concertos.

K. 218 in D major is the fourth of Mozart's five great violin concertos and is one which has remained very much a part of the familiar violin repertoire. This work bears definite relation to a violin concerto in D major by Boccherini, composed ten years earlier, which Mozart may have heard in Florence in 1770 by his youthful friend, Thomas Linley, an English violinist and composer studying in Italy at that time. The two concertos have almost the same structure, and their thematic materials contain more than coincidental similarity. The assumption is, therefore, that the themes and much of the figuration lay dormant in Mozart's mind after his encounter with the Boccherini composition until the time arose five years later when he was to write his D major violin concerto. Mozart himself referred to this concerto in a letter to his father as the "Strasbourg Concerto," probably alluding to the musette motive in the last movement which may be derived from a Strassburg folk melody. A contemporary symphony by Karl von Dittersdorf contained a similar motive called the "ballo Strasburghese."

The first movement of K. 218 is in Classic concerto-sonata form, and this *Allegro* begins to reveal, even at a comparatively early stage of Mozart's development, some of the ingenuity, the originality, and the expert craftsmanship which make his piano concertos masterpieces of form which have never been surpassed. Mozart's concerto form is never stereotyped and no two concertos are ever alike in their thematic organization. Mozart seems to delight in continual surprises, for the listener can never be sure which themes from the opening tutti the soloist will use, which themes will not be heard again at all, or what new material will be introduced during the course of the movement. It is Mozart's unique treatment of the subject matter in his concertos that makes these works marvels of formal construction.

K. 218 opens with a bold repeated-note theme in the orchestra.

Example 1. Mozart, Violin Concerto in D major, K. 218, First Movement.

The second half of the theme is stated in a more subdued tone by the violins over a repeated-note accompaniment.

Example 2. Mozart, Violin Concerto in D major, K. 218, First Movement.

The second subject appears (Example 3) and is followed by an extended passage which is almost of sufficient importance to be considered a separate theme in itself (Example 4).

Example 3. Mozart, Violin Concerto in D major, K. 218, First Movement.

Example 4. Mozart, Violin Concerto in D major, K. 218, First Movement.

The solo violin enters immediately with a restatement of the opening tutti material. The rhythmic motive of the opening theme is carried on by the horns and sometimes the oboes throughout the movement, but this opening subject never returns after its two statements in the exposition. Following the principal subject, the solo violin then introduces a new theme (Example 5) and continues with an extensive bridge section which leads to the dominant key and the second subject.

Example 5. Mozart, Violin Concerto in D major, K. 218, First Movement.

The closing material is played by the orchestra alone with the solo violin entering again at the beginning of the development section.

The development is comparatively short, consisting of only thirty measures, and the material is based on the orchestral accompaniment of the principal theme as found in measures 8-10. The solo violin leads from the development immediately to the recapitulation, but rather than using the principal subject as might be expected, Mozart introduces the recapitulation with the new theme (Example 5) which was inserted in the exposition between the first and second subjects. This theme is followed by bridge material similar to that heard in the exposition which leads to the second subject, stated this time in the tonic key. The continuation of the second subject is varied only slightly from the comparable material heard in the exposition and is separated from the closing section by the cadenza. The closing section is again played by the orchestra alone, and the movement ends with repeated "d's" in dotted rhythm, reminiscent of the opening measures of the concerto.

The second movement, *Andante Cantabile*, begins with a short orchestral statement of the principal theme.

Example 6. Mozart, Violin Concerto in D major, K. 218, Second Movement.

After the entrance of the solo violin the movement becomes an uninterrupted song for violin, the melodic flow pausing only once to allow a short cadenza.

The final movement of K. 218 is a rondeau: *Andante grazioso*. Mozart's use of the rondeau, or the French equivalent of the rondo, suggests that he was familiar with some of the representatives of the French violin school such as Le Duc and Guenin. Mozart, however, combines both French and Italian influences in this work, interpolating episodes such as the gavotte and musette section which would be familar to his audiences. As mentioned earlier, the musette section of this particular movement was referred to in the Mozart correspondence as probably originating in Strassburg.

The solo violin enters with the orchestra at the beginning of the movement and continues to play until the very last measure.

Example 7.   Mozart, Violin Concerto in D major, K. 218, Third Movement.

Piano Concerto in E-Flat Major, K. 271

Demonstrating a huge stride in Mozart's artistic development is the Piano Concerto in E-flat major, K. 271. It is the first of Mozart's concertos to be considered a masterpiece, and correctly so, for in this work may be seen the first evidence of a deepening musical maturity. Mozart composed this concerto in January, 1777, in Salzburg. It was written for Mlle. Jeunehomme, a lady virtuoso from Paris who had an excellent reputation as a performer. In this respect alone it differs from the earlier concertos which, with the exception of K. 238, were composed for much less competent performers. Mozart must have felt unrestricted from a musical standpoint as well, for the work differs from its predecessors as much in its depth of expression as in its greater technical freedom. The first striking feature is its beginning. The piano enters in the second measure and shares the initial statement of the theme with the orchestra.

Orchestra   Piano

Example 8.   Mozart, Piano Concerto in E-flat major, K. 271, First Movement.

This early entrance of the piano before the customary orchestral tutti is the delightful experiment of a composer whose imagination set out to do something different. Mozart does not abolish the opening tutti, for as soon as the piano has affirmed its presence, the orchestra proceeds with its normal task of introducing the themes. It is curious that Mozart never again began a concerto in this same way. Perhaps this example of his unconventionality is all the more intriguing because of its uniqueness.

The first movement of K. 271 contains a wealth of musical ideas, and Mozart's ingenious treatment of the material is everywhere evident. The alternation of themes throughout the movement and the constant interplay between solo and orchestra are especially noteworthy. One time the solo will state the first half of a theme and the orchestra the second part; at the next occurrence the order will be reversed. All the themes in the movement, except the opening flourish of the piano, are found in the orchestral tutti.

Following the opening measures in which piano and orchestra state the main subject in dialogue, the orchestra continues with this melody:

Example 9.   Mozart, Piano Concerto in E-flat major, K. 271, First Movement.

The second theme, which the piano presents in the dominant key during the exposition, is stated first in the key of the tonic by the orchestra.

Example 10.   Mozart, Piano Concerto in E-flat major, K. 271, First Movement.

The second movement of K. 271 is one of Mozart's most expressive and deeply moving *Andantinos*. It is in the key of C minor, a key which Mozart consistently used in many of his most profound compositions. Clearly influenced by the opera, this movement is itself an instrumental aria. Muted strings present the contemplative principal theme:

Example 11.   Mozart, Piano Concerto in E-flat major, K. 271, Second Movement.

The final movement of K. 271 is a rondo with a menuetto interpolated. The rondo, a form carried over from the Baroque suite, was frequently used as the form of the final movement of sonatas and con-

certos in Classic music. Mozart, in his treatment of the rondo, raised
the form to a higher level of organization than it had previously known.
Neither his sonata movements nor his rondo movements are stereotyped. Each rondo is slightly different in design from the others, for
in these movements Mozart varies the order of themes and causes them
to appear in surprising places. The rondos show an affinity for sonata
form when a development section occurs (rondo-sonata); also Mozart
rondos frequently contain slow sections and cadenzas.

The piano opens the movement with a highly organized refrain
which the orchestra immediately takes up:

Example 12.   Mozart, Piano Concerto in E-flat major, K. 271, Third
              Movement.

Example 13 becomes a sprightly dialogue between piano and orchestra.

Example 13.   Mozart, Piano Concerto in E-flat major, K. 271, Third
              Movement.

The secondary theme is given to the piano alone:

Example 14.   Mozart, Piano Concerto in E-flat major, K. 271, Third
              Movement.

There are three cadenzas in this movement in addition to the lovely
Menuetto, which, with its graceful melodies and *pizzicato* orchestral
accompaniment, offers some of the most delightful moments in the
entire concerto.

Example 15.   Mozart, Piano Concerto in E-flat major, K. 271, Third
              Movement.

With the exception of the Menuetto, this rondo is a grand perpetual motion. The only other concerto finale comparable to it is the last movement of the Piano Concerto in A major, K. 488. Mozart rarely gives the soloist any periods of rest or inactivity, but instead builds up a rhythmic and melodic drive which is relieved only by the final chord. K. 271, a masterpiece which some scholars believe Mozart never surpassed, foreshadowed the later great Vienna concertos and established the young composer as a mature musician.

A characteristic feature of the solo concerto and the Classic concerto in particular is that section known as the cadenza. Occurring usually near the close of the first movement, but not restricted to this location, the cadenza belongs entirely to the soloist. The orchestra comes to rest leaving the soloist in command of the complete attention of the audience. Originally associated with the abilities of the composer and not merely with the facility of the performer, the cadenza provided a vehicle for the spontaneous creative genius of the composer-performer (nearly always the same person).

Incontestably, the ability to improvise reached its height of expression in the cadenza sections of the solo concertos of Mozart and Beethoven. Many of their contemporaries have attested to the sheer wonder of hearing these masters perform extemporaneously, so the cadenza would have been the high point of the concerto for an audience sensitive to the tremendous musical demands which extemporaneous improvisation makes upon the soloist. After Mozart and Beethoven, though, the division between composer and performer became so prominent that the art of improvisation was lost, and with the disappearance of this art, the value of the cadenza diminished until its original purpose was forgotten. The importance of the cadenza today is associated entirely with the virtuosity of the performer who plays a previously composed cadenza either by the composer or by some other person who has attempted to recreate the composer's style.

Mozart once wrote to his father concerning a cadenza for the D major Piano Concerto, K. 175: ". . . when I play the concerto I always put in whatever occurs to me."[8] Since Mozart did not need to write his cadenzas down, except for the use of students or friends, there are a sparse number of Mozart cadenzas for his concertos. Even those which do exist are most certainly not as Mozart himself played them, and, for some of his greatest piano concertos, Mozart left no cadenzas at all. Those cadenzas which are available have been collected together under the Köchel number 624.

Piano Concerto in A Major, K. 488

The Piano Concerto in A major, K. 488, is the first of three concertos written in the year 1786. A hauntingly beautiful work, its first
movement bears closer similarity to the sonata-form regularity of text-
book description than is usual in Mozart. The main theme is first declared by the orchestra and is repeated by the piano at its entrance:

Example 16.   Mozart, Piano Concerto in A major, K. 488, First
Movement.

In similar fashion, the orchestra presents the melody which the piano
later repeats as the secondary subject:

Example 17.   Mozart, Piano Concerto in A major, K. 488, First
Movement.

Rarely does Mozart permit the solo such as a straightforward repetition
of themes found in the orchestral tutti. More frequently the melodies
are reshuffled in the first solo and reorganized throughout the movement
so that the order of appearance is never quite certain. Just when it
seems that Mozart is at last resorting to a "normal" sonata-form movement, the orchestra stops short, pauses for half a measure, then resumes
with a quiet new theme upon which the development section is based:

Example 18.   Mozart, Piano Concerto in A major, K. 488, First
Movement.

The recapitulation proceeds with the regularity of the exposition, until,
after the presentation of the secondary subject, the piano stops abruptly,
pauses for half a measure, and repeats the new theme of the development section, exchanging places with the orchestra for this final appearance.

The music of Mozart is not often mournful. Expressive, tender, somber—yes, but it was not in keeping with the philosophy under which Mozart worked to let such feelings as true pathos or melancholia creep into his music. Though well acquainted with these emotions and those conditions which produce them, Mozart was skilled in the personal discipline of sublimating his own sensations for the broader expression of universal suffering. The second movement of K. 488, *Adagio,* is an exception to this philosophy, and a personal feeling of utter despondency is the tragic keynote of this remarkable piece. In F-sharp minor, a rare choice of keys for Mozart, the movement plumbs emotional depths with profound insight. The principal theme, with its singing melody, is given to the piano alone,

Example 19.   Mozart, Piano Concerto in A major, K. 488, Second Movement.

while the orchestra presents still another theme at its initial entrance:

Example 20.   Mozart, Piano Concerto in A major, K. 488, Second Movement.

Deeply satisfying in its intense beauty, the movement seems to end too soon.

As if in an effort to erase the sadness of the previous movement from mind, the rondo betrays no trace of gloom as it cavorts merrily from one sprightly theme to another. Remarkable in its absolute contrast from the *Adagio,* the rondo is, like the finale of K. 271, a grand perpetual motion, and demands great agility from the performer. The piano enters with the first of many themes:

Example 21.   Mozart, Piano Concerto in A major, K. 488, Third Movement.

The second principal subject is also given to the piano,

Example 22. Mozart, Piano Concerto in A major, K. 488, Third Movement.

while the orchestra introduces the third:

Example 23. Mozart, Piano Concerto in A major, K. 488, Third Movement.

Other subsidiary themes combine with those illustrated to make this a delightful, captivating finale.

Piano Concerto in C Minor, K. 491

After hearing a performance of Mozart's Piano Concerto in C minor, K. 491, Beethoven once remarked, "Ah! we shall never be able to do anything like that."[9] Composed just three weeks after the great A major Concerto, K. 488, and scarcely a month before the completion of *The Marriage of Figaro*, the monumental C minor Concerto shows no signs of haste nor evidence of the pressures which must surely have harassed Mozart during its composition. Unparalleled among concertos of its time, it remains one of Mozart's finest contributions in the instrumental field. K. 491 is a monument of musical architecture as timeless and as moving as a great cathedral or priceless piece of sculpture.

The opening theme begins softly in the orchestra, but there is a reserve of power in the broad phrases and the wide leaps which soon breaks out into the full orchestral sound.

Example 24. Mozart, Piano Concerto in C minor, K. 491, First Movement.

There are at least five themes in the long orchestral tutti, but when the piano enters, it uses none of these. Playing alone, the piano voices a completely new melody:

Example 25.   Mozart, Piano Concerto in C minor, K. 491, First
Movement.

Though the solo states the last part of the opening subject shortly after
its entrance, it never presents the entire main theme (Example 24) at
any time. Another new melody, the second subject, does not occur in
the opening tutti:

Example 26.   Mozart, Piano Concerto in C minor, K. 491, First
Movement.

In the coda, both solo and orchestra maintain a pedal point of "c"
while the piano plays arpeggios in a rhythmic allusion to the main
theme. There is no final statement, in the coda, of any of the themes
from the movement.

The simplicity of the second movement of K. 491, a *Larghetto* in
E-flat major, provides welcome relief from the powerful drama of the
opening movement. Retaining all the instruments used in the preceding
movement, Mozart uses them with such skillful balance that the effect
never destroys the serenity of this rondo movement. There is a second
section in C minor and a third in A-flat major, while the main theme
always appears in the key of the movement:

Example 27.   Mozart, Piano Concerto in C minor, K. 491, Second
Movement.

The finale consists of a theme with eight variations, a work which
returns to the massive tonal effects of the first movement. The theme
itself is somber and almost gruff, with short, two-note phrases adding
to the effect:

Example 28.   Mozart, Piano Concerto in C minor, K. 491, Third
Movement.

Representing many moods, the variations make use of different techniques as well: triplets, contrapuntal writing, changes of key, and finally a change to the 6/8 rhythm in which the movement ends.

K. 491 uses a larger orchestra than any of Mozart's works in concerto form. More heavily scored than either the G minor or the C major ("Jupiter") symphonies, the work requires one flute, two oboes, two clarinets, two bassoons, two horns, two trumpets, and drums.

Mozart's intense activity in the field of the piano concerto did not preclude work on concertos for other media. Reference has been made previously to the five violin concertos. There are also concertos for wind instruments, ranging from early compositions to the Clarinet Concerto in A major, K. 622, Mozart's last work in concerto form. The first concerto for a wind instrument is the Bassoon Concerto in B-flat major, K. 191, written in 1774. For the flute, an instrument of which he was not fond, Mozart composed two concertos—the G major Concerto, K. 313, and the D major Concerto, K. 314. Both works were written for instrumentalists of Mozart's acquaintance. For his Salzburg friend, Ignaz Leitgeb, who played the horn, Mozart composed three concertos—K. 417, K. 447, and K. 495—all in the key of E-flat major. There is also the D major Horn Concerto, K. 412, whose movements probably were originally separate pieces rather than a single composition. The Concerto for Flute and Harp in C major, K. 299, was written in Paris for the Duc de Guines and his daughter. Neither of the instruments was a particular favorite of Mozart but he did respect the abilities of his performers and the result is a delightful, though not elaborate, concerto in Gallic style.

The Mozart concertos represent the epitome of the Classic concerto style and the point of departure for every later composer of concertos. All the intricacies, subtleties, and countless possibilities inherent in the form were fully developed by Mozart. Particularly unique in concerto literature are the twenty-four piano concertos. Johannes Brahms, the great nineteenth-century composer who was himself a composer of concertos, once wrote of them:

> That people in general do not understand and do not respect the greatest things, such as Mozart's concertos, helps our kind to live and acquire renown. If they would only know that they are getting from us by drops what they could drink there to their hearts' content![10]

BASIC LISTENING:

MOZART, Violin Concerto in D Major, K. 218
———, Piano Concerto in E-flat major, K. 271
———, Piano Concerto in A major, K. 488
———, Piano Concerto in C minor, K. 491

ADDITIONAL SUGGESTED LISTENING:

BACH, C. P. E., Violoncello Concerto in A major
BACH, J. C., Cembalo Concerto in B-flat major, Op. 13, No. 4
HAYDN, CLAVIER Concerto in D major, Op. 21
MOZART, Piano Concerto in B-flat major, K. 450
——, Piano Concerto in D minor, K. 466
——, Piano Concerto in C major, K. 467
——, Piano Concerto in E-flat major, K. 482
——, Piano Concerto in B-flat major, K. 595

ADDITIONAL READING:

BLOM, ERIC, *Mozart*. London: J. M. Dent and Sons, 1935.
EINSTEIN, ALFRED, *Mozart: His Character, His Work*. Translated by Arthur Mendel and Nathan Broder. London: Oxford University Press, 1945. (See Chapter 17: The Synthesis: The Clavier Concerto).
GEIRINGER, KARL, *Haydn*. Second Edition. New York: Doubleday & Co., Inc., 1963. An Anchor book.
GROUT, DONALD JAY, *A History of Western Music*. New York: W. W. Norton & Company, Inc., 1960. (See pp. 411-426).
TURNER, W. J., *Mozart: The Man and His Works*. New York: Alfred A. Knopf, 1945.

FOOTNOTES

[1]Paul Henry Lang, *Music in Western Civilization* (New York: W. W. Norton and Company, Inc., 1941), p. 639.
[2]Hans Mersman, *Letters of Wolfgang Amadeus Mozart,* translated by M. M. Bozman (London: J. M. Dent & Sons, Ltd., 1928), p. 9.
[3]*Ibid.,* p. 23.
[4]*Ibid.,* p. 21.
[5]*Ibid.,* p. 68.
[6]Leo Smith, *Music of the Seventeenth and Eighteenth Centuries* (London: J. M. Dent & Sons, Ltd., 1931), p. 221.
[7]*Loc. cit.*
[8]Mersman, *op. cit.,* pp. 221-213.
[9]W. J. Turner, *Mozart: The Man and His Works* (New York: Alfred A. Knopf, 1945), p. 134.
[10]Lang, *op. cit.,* p. 904.

beethoven
and the concerto

In deference to his unique position in music history and because of his formidable contribution to music literature, it is necessary to place Beethoven in a chapter apart, and indeed, it seems certain that he would have preferred such treatment. A man bound to the past yet standing on the threshold of new ideas and new ways to express those ideas, Beethoven remains deeply rooted in the Classic musical tradition even as the stirring of Romanticism may be seen in his work. In an age when man struggles for freedom, independence, and dignity, Beethoven is a kindred spirit. For Beethoven acknowledged no master and was servant to no man.

While Mozart composed in a seemingly effortless stream of creativity, Beethoven composed in a tortuous, self-disciplined fashion. His brusque, outspoken, and unrefined nature was the very antithesis of the courtly drawing-room and salon atmosphere. Yet his bombastic and gruff manner disguised a sensitive soul racked with loneliness, grief, and the keen dread of deafness, the affliction which eventually separated him from the rest of the world.

Beethoven was a musical giant, and he worked as a giant would, with boldness and intrepidity. His dauntless pen lashed out as his doughty tongue frequently did, creating, in tone and color, the musical expression of his personality. Beethoven neither composed for demanding patron nor for the unpredictable public. He permitted only his own stringently critical standard to be the master of his art.

Beethoven's major compositions in concerto form are six in number: five for the piano and one for the violin.* Though Beethoven's concerto compositions do not span his lifetime as do those of Mozart, there is still such stylistic difference between the first and last of these works that it is impossible not to see the musical personality of Beethoven emerging with explosive intensity.

Beethoven's first concertos, No. 1 in C major, Op. 15, and No. 2 in B-flat major, Op. 19, both for piano, are concertos which Beethoven later described as "not among my best works in this form."[1] The composer's remarks should not be misinterpreted to mean that these concertos are musically poor, for Beethoven would never have permitted the publication of any composition he truly felt was inferior. Still feeling his way in the concerto idiom, Beethoven had not yet approached the mastery of both form and content which his later concertos reveal. The B-flat Concerto, No. 2, actually composed at an earlier date than the Concerto No. 1 in C major, is strongly Mozartean in conception, verifying the high esteem and reverence in which Beethoven held the older master. From the C major Concerto come suggestions of the vigorous individual characteristics typical of the mature Beethoven style, but the influence of his recent teacher, Haydn, is also in great evidence. Not until the Concerto No. 3 in C minor, Op. 37, did Beethoven indicate satisfaction with his efforts in this realm.

PIANO CONCERTO NO. 3 IN C MINOR, OP. 37

The Third Piano Concerto, composed in 1800, was begun, though possibly not completely finished, during the summer when Beethoven had left the city to spend a period of time in the peaceful environment of the country. When he returned to Vienna after such intervals of refreshment, Beethoven always brought with him some significant composition written during his absence from the city. The Third Piano Concerto is such a work.

Beethoven did not give the premiere performance of his Third Concerto until April 5, 1803, and publication was delayed until 1804.

---

*Mention should be made of the Triple Concerto for Piano, Violin, Violoncello and Orchestra, Op. 56, which was written in 1805 but was performed in public only once during Beethoven's lifetime. Though the work possesses some measure of greatness, it is generally considered not to have achieved the high level of the piano concertos and the violin concerto. At the age of thirteen, Beethoven composed a piano concerto undiscovered for a long period of time but now published together with other supplemental works. The first movement of an unfinished piano concerto in D major, found years after Beethoven's death, is another early attempt at concerto writing. In the sketchbooks for the year 1815, long after Beethoven had written his last piano concerto, are found sketches of another piano concerto in D major, only one of many works which Beethoven left incomplete.

The work appeared on a concert program featuring Beethoven's music together with the first and second symphonies, the oratorio, "Christus am Ölberge," and several other shorter works which were finally omitted at the actual performance due to the extreme length of the program. Ignatz von Seyfried, a friend of Beethoven and also a conductor, composer and musician, gives an amusing account of the first performance of the Third Piano Concerto:

> At the performance of the Concerto he asked me to turn the pages for him; but—heaven help me!— that was easier said than done. I saw almost nothing but empty leaves; at the most on one page or the other a few Egyptian hieroglyphs wholly unintelligible to me scribbled down to serve as clues for him; for he played nearly all of the solo part from memory. . . . He gave me a secret glance whenever he was at the end of one of the invisible passages and my scarcely concealable anxiety not to miss the decisive moment amused him greatly and he laughed heartily at the jovial supper which we ate afterwards.[2]

Ferdinand Ries, Beethoven's pupil, played the concerto at a concert in July, 1804. He writes: "Beethoven had given me his beautiful Concerto in C minor (Op. 37) in manuscript so that I might make my first public appearance *as his pupil* with it; and I am the only one who ever appeared as such while Beethoven was alive."[3] Ries further comments: "The pianoforte part of the C minor Concerto *was never completely written out* in the score; Beethoven wrote it down on separate sheets of paper expressly for me."[4] This would confirm Seyfried's earlier experience with the scribbled markings from which Beethoven played the work at the initial performance. The young student urged Beethoven to write a cadenza for the concerto which he could use at his performance, but Beethoven refused and instead ordered Ries to compose one of his own. The cadenza received only a few minor corrections from Beethoven, but it was so difficult that Ries had trouble playing it without floundering. Finally, just prior to the concert, Beethoven angrily ordered Ries to change the section which he could not play properly. When the moment came in the actual performance for the cadenza, the young pianist could not bring himself to play the easier one and as he began the difficult version "Beethoven violently jerked his chair."[5] Fortunately, Ries played the cadenza this time both to his and Beethoven's satisfaction, and Beethoven was so pleased that he shouted "Bravo!" Ries says, "This electrified the entire audience and at once gave me a standing among the artists. Afterward, while expressing his satisfaction he (Beethoven) added: 'But all the same you are willful!— If you had made a slip in the passage I would never have given you another lesson.' "[6]

The Third Concerto is stylistically advanced over the two earlier concertos. Gone are the Mozartean or Haydnesque touches which marked the C major and B-flat concertos. This work reveals the composer at the threshold of his powers as a mature musician. In the first movement, with its formal problems and the challenge of the delicate balance between solo and orchestra, Beethoven takes a step forward away from the symphonic conception and closer to the unsurpassed solution which Mozart had attained for his opening orchestral tuttis.

The first movement, *Allegro con brio,* begins softly in the orchestra with a somber, almost foreboding theme. The first phrase is stated by the strings alone, the second in a higher register by the winds, achieving a question-and-answer effect of quiet impressiveness:

Example 1. Beethoven, Piano Concerto No. 3, Op. 37, First Movement.

By means of a short series of chords in harmonic sequence, Beethoven modulates into the presentation of the principal theme in the key of E-flat, continuing on to the introduction of the second subject in the same tonality:

Example 2. Beethoven, Piano Concerto No. 3, Op. 37, First Movement.

After the second subject has been heard, rather than allowing the orchestra to stray into episodic passages as in the first two concertos, and as would be proper in the first movement of a symphony, Beethoven modulates abruptly to the key of C major with another statement of the second theme and returns the orchestra immediately to the C minor tonality and to the closing themes before the opening tutti is able to turn into a miniature symphonic movement. In this concerto, Beethoven begins to approach Mozart's understanding of the opening tutti: that the purpose of the tutti is to prepare for the entrance of the solo, not to present a symphonic exposition.

When the piano enters, it prefaces its statement of the principal theme with three measures of unison scale passages, each in a successively higher register, a dramatic touch of Beethoven's genius. The piano plays alone for some bars, then proceeds into expansive material in which Beethoven makes prominent use of triplet and two-against-three rhythms. The piano presents the second subject in E-flat, then digresses into sparkling passage work from which the orchestra emerges to bring the exposition to a close, but not in the expected key of the movement. The exposition ends, and the development section begins in the key of D major, then proceeds immediately into G minor. The piano initiates the development with the same dramatic scales which marked its first appearance, but the spirit of the music changes abruptly and the main subject is developed in a *cantabile* style. Beethoven dramatically builds up the return of the C minor tonality and the restatement of the principal theme, and the recapitulation begins *fortissimo* in the orchestra. The first section of the recapitulation is very much shortened and the dramatic scale passages in the piano are omitted. The second subject returns in C major and after additional passage work in the piano, the orchestra leads to the cadenza. Ordinarily, the orchestra brings the movement to a close following the cadenza, but in this concerto, Beethoven permits the piano to play throughout the entire coda. The scale passages, not repeated at the beginning of the recapitulation, signal the end of the movement with one brilliant sweep up the keyboard.

The *Largo* movement is the most complex of all the slow movements in Beethoven's piano concertos. It belongs almost entirely to the piano alone, for the orchestra is used principally for accompaniment and for rhythmic punctuation from time to time. The movement is in E major, an unusual relationship to the C minor of the first movement. The opening theme is stated in a homophonic texture but the solo part soon becomes florid and melismatic in its treatment of the theme.

Example 3.   Beethoven, Piano Concerto No. 3, Op. 37, Second Movement.

The piano spins ornate figures with arpeggios, double thirds, scales, and tremolos, but after a short cadenza the piano returns to the simpler style of the opening bars to end the movement.

The finale is a rondo in the grand manner, a commanding and vivacious piece. The spirited opening theme portrays the vigor and enthusiasm of the composer:

Example 4. Beethoven, Piano Concerto No. 3, Op. 37, Third Movement.

By the time Beethoven had published the Third Concerto, he had become a well-established and sought-after musician in Vienna. There were more demands for his music than he could satisfy and, between his publications and his appearances as a performing artist, he was able to realize enough financial reward to live independently and fairly comfortably. His greatest trial was the state of his health. Throughout much of his lifetime he suffered from severe intestinal difficulties during which he often subjected himself to drastic measures in hope of effecting a cure. His hearing began to disintegrate when he was not yet thirty. The shock of realizing the inevitability of deafness upon such a man is hardly comprehensible. As early as 1801 Beethoven confided to a few friends that his hearing was being affected:

> . . . my ears whistle and buzz continually, day and night. I can say I am living a wretched life; for two years I have avoided almost all social gatherings because it is impossible for me to say to people: I am deaf. If I belonged to any other profession it would be easier, but in my profession it is an awful state.[7]

Though some allowance must be made for the possibility that Beethoven may have exaggerated somewhat the severity of his infirmity at this time, records do exist which prove that his hearing was definitely impaired by the summer of 1801 and the affliction progressed surely, if not swiftly, toward total deafness. Even during the last few years of his life, Beethoven still sought after physicians who were known to be experienced in ear physiology, although he quickly grew impatient with methods and treatments when there was no immediate improvement. Eventually he was forced to carry on conversations with the aid of a pad and pencil. Though proud, sensitive, and ill at ease, sometime during his own private battle with the realization of his fate Beethoven resolved that "it shall not wholly overcome me."[8] And indeed, it did not.

PIANO CONCERTO NO. 5 IN E-FLAT MAJOR, OP. 73

During the spring of 1809, war between France and Austria became imminent and apparently unavoidable. In May the Empress and the

Imperial family left Vienna accompanied by Archduke Rudolph, Beethoven's friend, pupil, and benefactor. As a token of mourning, Beethoven wrote the first movement of the Piano Sonata, Op. 81a. In August Napoleon's forces began firing on Vienna and almost immediately secured a surrender of Archduke Maximilian's defenders. The subsequent occupation of Vienna by the French forced Beethoven's confinement within the city during the summer season when he was ordinarily fond of retiring to the country. During this troubled time Beethoven undoubtedly completed Op. 81a and in all probability also finished the Fifth Piano Concerto. The Concerto, Piano Sonata, Op. 81a, and the Quartet, Op. 74 ("The Harp") were all projected at approximately the same time and all were written in the same key—E-flat major.

Dedicated to Archduke Rudolph, the Fifth Piano Concerto was published in 1811 and first performed by Johann Schneider during that year, in Leipzig, where it enjoyed great success. It was reported that the concerto put the audience into such "a state of enthusiasm that it could hardly content itself with the ordinary expressions of recognition and enjoyment."[9] The work was first played in Vienna in 1812 where its reception was somewhat less enthusiastic. The occasion was a benefit of the Society of Noble Ladies for Charity which also featured an exhibition of paintings by Raphael, Poussin, and Troyes. Played by Beethoven's pupil, Carl Czerny, this performance was a total failure. "The reason," explained a perceptive contemporary reviewer, "is to be sought partly in the subjective character of the work, partly in the objective nature of the listeners. Beethoven, full of proud confidence in himself, never writes for the multitudes. He demands understanding and feeling, and because of the intentional difficulties he can receive these only at the hands of the knowing, a majority of whom is not to be found on such occasions."[10]

Although Beethoven himself gave the premiere performances of each of the other piano concertos, it is not known whether he ever played the Fifth Concerto in public. By the date of its publication his deafness had virtually brought to an end his concert appearances. The early termination of his pianistic career may well have been a factor in Beethoven's withdrawal from further concerto composition, for though he lived nearly twenty years after completing the Fifth Concerto, he never again turned to the concerto idiom for the expression of his musical creativity.

Beethoven varies the customary concerto routine again in this work and begins not with the usual tutti but with an introduction in which the piano plays by far the more prominent part. In the orchestral tutti following the introduction, the principal themes are set forth in logical sequence. The principal theme:

Example 5.   Beethoven, Piano Concerto No. 5, Op. 73, First Movement.

The second subject:

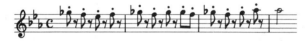

Example 6.   Beethoven, Piano Concerto No. 5, Op. 73, First Movement.

There are, in addition to these, a wealth of other themes in these opening measures leading to and preparing for the entry of the piano for the first solo. Beginning with a long chromatic scale, the piano restates the principal subject and joins the orchestra in the exposition of the other themes already set forth in the opening tutti. When the piano enters again in the development, its entry is once more marked by the long chromatic scale which now leads to a development of the principal subject based on both the melodic contour and the rhythmic pattern of the theme. The development is climaxed by a series of octave passages in the piano part which covers the entire range of the keyboard. There follows an expressive reappearance of the closing theme. Beginning with the introductory material heard at the beginning of the movement, the recapitulation progresses with the customary restatement of the two main subjects. Beethoven, whose dramatic sense of key relationship has been noted previously, uses the unusual tonal center of C-sharp minor for the return of the second theme, proceeding quickly then into D-flat major and back again into the key of the tonic (E-flat).

In all the earlier concertos, Beethoven reserved the usual place at the close of the recapitulation for a cadenza during which, if he were soloist, he would improvise, as did many other prominent pianists of the time, or a soloist could also use a written cadenza supplied by the composer. In this concerto Beethoven deviates from the scheme and writes out the cadenza, or more aptly a coda, as an integral part of the movement. Beethoven had previously permitted the piano to play with the orchestra following the cadenza to the very final bars, as in the Third and Fourth Concertos, but this is the first Classic concerto to omit the established cadenza in favor of one massive coda at the conclusion of the first movement. The chromatic scales which have announced the entry of the piano twice before in the movement now herald the lengthy trills which lead immediately to the agitated closing.

The second movement, *Adagio un poco moto*, leads directly to the final movement. Written in the key of B major, the slow movement again illustrates Beethoven's predilection for unorthodox tonal relationships. There are two themes; the first is stated by the orchestra with muted violins over a *pizzicato* bass:

Example 7. Beethoven, Piano Concerto No. 5, Op. 73, Second Movement.

The piano enters with the second theme, a melody in triplet figures:

Example 8. Beethoven, Piano Concerto No. 5, Op. 73, Second Movement.

Returning in the piano part, the first theme shifts back again to the orchestra while the piano provides an ornamental accompaniment which diminishes gradually until all that remains is a single tonic note, "b." Pizzicato strings alter this down a half step to "b-flat" and the piano, still in *adagio* tempo, enters now in the key of E-flat major with the hesitant but unmistakable new theme of the final movement, or rondo.

With this daring modulation, the tempo becomes *allegro,* and the rondo is at once in full progress. The main theme, hinted at in the closing moments of the slow movement, now makes a full appearance in the piano part.

Example 9. Beethoven, Piano Concerto No. 5, Op. 73, Third Movement.

Other musical ideas enter, but they are never given the prominence of this principal subject. The rhythmic figure ♩.♫ ♫♫ is also particularly conspicuous not only within the movement proper but also in the final bars of the coda where the timpani and piano are the only instruments heard. This monumental rondo is a fitting conclusion to Beethoven's last piano concerto.

VIOLIN CONCERTO IN D MAJOR, OP. 61

The Violin Concerto, the only solo concerto Beethoven composed for any instrument other than the piano, was written for a violin virtuoso named Franz Clement. On the manuscript Beethoven inscribed the work to Clement with a pun on his "clemency" toward the composer! Beethoven finished the concerto in 1806 just in time for the performance, making it necessary for Clement to read the music at sight without previous rehearsal. It is hardly surprising that the concerto made no lasting impression at this occasion, though the work is among the finest of the violin concertos in the repertoire.

The rhythmic motive for the entire first movement is contained in the muffled timpani strokes which precede the entrance of the main theme in the woodwinds:

Example 10.   Beethoven, Violin Concerto, Op. 61, First Movement.

A scale theme, stated first by the orchestra, gains further importance later in the solo violin:

Example 11.   Beethoven, Violin Concerto, Op. 61, First Movement.

Another subsidiary theme, of bombastic quality, enters with a sudden *fortissimo*:

Example 12.   Beethoven, Violin Concerto, Op. 61, First Movement.

Supported again by the rhythmic figure first heard in the timpani but now in the strings, the second subject enters, a lovely melody in the brightly-colored woodwinds:

Example 13.   Beethoven, Violin Concerto, Op. 61, First Movement.

The solo entry is well prepared by the majestic closing theme of the tutti:

Example 14.   Beethoven, Violin Concerto, Op. 61, First Movement.

The violin makes its first appearance with a lengthy introduction before it continues into the thematic exposition of the first solo. It is the development section which is unusual in this *Allegro* and which broadens the movement out into gigantic proportions. Beginning the section with Example 12, the orchestra proceeds into the second subject and from there into what is almost a second exposition. The violin enters with similar but extended introductory material such as marked its initial appearance, leading, as before, to a development of the principal theme. Suddenly, in the middle of the development, a new theme appears, a *cantabile* melody in the key of G minor, with the rhythmic motif clearly discernible in the accompaniment of the horns and bassoons. The music remains quietly subdued as the violin, mounting higher and higher in broken-chord figures, maneuvers with characteristic skill back into the key of the tonic and into the principal subject. Reappearances of the subordinate themes follow, together with the second subject and the closing theme.

It is almost certain that Clement supplied his own cadenza for this concerto, for there is none extant from Beethoven's pen. Two equally prominent violinists have written adequate cadenzas for the work, Joseph Joachim and Fritz Kreisler, and one of these is usually performed in the accustomed place. Following the cadenza, the violin momentarily reminisces on the second subject before the closing theme is heard softly and the violin ascends in a rapid *crescendo* to end the movement.

The second movement, *Larghetto*, is a theme and variations in which the mood is one of quiet composure. Muted strings present the theme first:

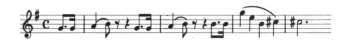

Example 15.   Beethoven, Violin Concerto, Op. 61, Second Movement.

Three variations follow, then an entirely new theme enters—an unusual procedure in this type of form.

Example 16.   Beethoven, Violin Concerto, Op. 61, Second Movement.

After a return to the original subject, the movement concludes with a brief cadenza by the violin and enters directly into the finale.

As though to balance the serenity of the preceding movement, the rondo is all light-heartedness and good humor and has a distinct folk quality in its principal theme:

Example 17.   Beethoven, Violin Concerto, Op. 61, Third Movement.

Resembling the call of the hunting horns, the transition theme appears:

Example 18.   Beethoven, Violin Concerto, Op. 61, Third Movement.

It is followed immediately by the second subject, stated in dialogue between the solo and orchestra:

Example 19.   Beethoven, Violin Concerto, Op. 61, Third Movement.

The third theme, now in the key of G minor, completes the procession
of musical ideas.

Example 20. Beethoven, Violin Concerto, Op. 61, Third Movement.

All but the third subject reappear in the recapitulation, after which
Beethoven again writes one of his massive codas. Highly virtuosic, this
section, comprised of brilliant arpeggios and scales in the solo part,
brings the movement to an energetic conclusion.

The concertos of Beethoven are highly significant in music history.
Through them it is possible to trace Beethoven's musical steps from the
youthful works, influenced by Haydn and Mozart, to the composer's
independent, mature style. Although Beethoven left his indelible imprint upon the concerto, his contributions, his innovations, and his altera-
tions were all within the framework of the Classic concerto form as
he had inherited it from his predecessors. Beethoven never abandoned
the principles of the eighteenth century ideal. In his first movements,
where the challenge of the Classic concerto form is most demanding
to the composer, Beethoven remained consistently faithful to the sonata-
allegro design. His concertos all contain the typical double exposition—
one for the orchestra and one for the orchestra and solo combined.
Beethoven did digress from the Mozartian practice of bringing the
opening orchestral tutti to a full close before the solo entered, for, in
Beethoven's concertos, the main theme is often preceded by rhapsodic
introductory material. In the Fourth Piano Concerto, Beethoven allows
the solo the unprecedented privilege of stating the principal theme
before the orchestra has been heard at all, but as the music continues
the requirements of the Classic concerto-sonata form are fulfilled and
Beethoven strays no further than this from its boundaries. In the Fifth
Piano Concerto and the Violin Concerto Beethoven connects the last
two movements, a step in the direction of complete continuity of musical
thought which, in the nineteenth century, resulted in the one-movement
concerto. Beethoven's key relationships and unusual modulations are
modifications of the more stereotyped tonal schemes used by earlier
concerto writers. But as a concerto composer Beethoven, nevertheless,
remains in the Classic tradition.

Though the concertos mirror Beethoven's changing musical personality, they do not reveal the entire spectrum of his musical creativity.

Only a study of works such as the late piano sonatas and last quartets completes the survey of Beethoven's musical evolution.

BASIC LISTENING:

Piano Concerto No. 3 in C minor, Op. 37
Piano Concerto No. 5 in E-flat major, Op. 73
Violin Concerto in D major, Op. 61

ADDITIONAL SUGGESTED LISTENING:

Piano Concerto No. 1 in C major, Op. 15
Piano Concerto No. 2 in B-flat major, Op. 19
Piano Concerto No. 4 in G major, Op. 58

ADDITIONAL READING:

TOVEY, DONALD F., *Essays in Musical Analysis*, Volume III, Concertos. London: Oxford University Press, 1937.

GROUT, DONALD JAY, *A History of Western Music*. New York: W. W. Norton & Company, Inc., 1960. Chapter XV.

FOOTNOTES

[1]Alexander Wheelock Thayer, *The Life of Ludwig van Beethoven*. Edited by Henry Edward Krehbiel. (New York: G. Schirmer, Inc., 1921), I, 185 and 287.

[2]*Ibid.*, II, 7.

[3]*Ibid.*, p. 30.

[4]*Loc. cit.*

[5]*Loc. cit.*

[6]*Loc. cit.*

[7]*Ibid.*, I, 300.

[8]*Ibid.*, pp 302-303.

[9]*Ibid.*, II, 160.

[10]*Ibid.*, p. 215.

the romantic concerto

In the nineteenth century the concerto underwent modification and experimentation under composers who experienced new problems created by the virtuoso performer, the enlarged orchestra, and the growing dissatisfaction with sonata form.

While the focus of musical activity in the eighteenth century revolved around the salon or drawing room of a noble patron, this activity in the nineteenth century moved to the concert hall. The orchestra increased in size and volume, the solo instruments were pushed to the limits of their potential, and composers were forced to write suitably for these changing conditions. Compositions of greater magnitude, commensurate with the new spatial element, became prevalent.

The favorite single instrument of the Romantic composer was the piano. The piano was popular both at home and in the concert hall; it suited the needs of both amateur and virtuoso. Because of its ability to compete with the powerful orchestra, the piano proved to be the favorite solo instrument among the Romantic composers who wrote concertos.

The disciplines and restrictions of Classic forms were either adapted to accommodate a particular musical idea or dispensed with altogether. The concerto, which had always possessed the contrast of two opposing forces, was, however, ideally suited for the great technical proficiency of the Romantic virtuoso. As a result, to many composers, the balance and structure of the form was of secondary importance to sensational effects in the orchestra and solo parts. To other composers, traditional examples of Mozart and Beethoven were the models. The composers of the Romantic period, highly emotional and individualistic, veered consciously away from the refinements of the Classic style and often struggled to fit their music into Classic molds. Greater freedom of both form and content became an ideal of the Romantic composer.

SPOHR, WEBER, AND BERLIOZ

Contributing to the expanding concerto literature were composers who brought diversified solutions to the problems inherent in the form. Ludwig Spohr (1784-1859), a violin virtuoso, and in that era second only to Paganini, wrote concertos for his instrument in which he exploited the virtuoso element to the definite subordination of all other concerto principles. Though educated and trained in the Classic tradition, Spohr nevertheless revealed new conceptions which were taking shape as the nineteenth century progressed further away from older musical doctrines. Spohr preferred the one-movement concerto, and his music is tinged with a slight touch of the melancholia which later descended full scale upon Romantic compositions.

Carl Maria von Weber (1786-1826) led piano music across the elusive bridge between the eighteenth and nineteenth centuries. A keyboard virtuoso of great reputation and a composer of keen talent, Weber was unfortunately incapable of emerging from the shadow of Mozart and Beethoven. Though he was almost an exact contemporary of Beethoven, Weber did not follow the style of the Classic master. In his works the strict disciplines of eighteenth-century composition were supplanted by a personal freedom of style. Ill at ease in sonata form, Weber struggled with it purely from a sense of duty, and in some works even omitted the usual first movement in order to avoid the encumbrances of the form.

Weber composed three piano concertos and a number of concertos for a variety of wind instruments. Written in 1821, his last piano concerto, the *Konzertstück* in F minor, is the most memorable of Weber's works in this realm. The piece confirms in no uncertain terms the unusual pianistic ability of its composer as it explores the possibilities of the piano in a virtuosic if shallow direction beyond the range of Beethoven's piano writing. In the *Konzertstück* Weber abandons any attempt to wrestle with sonata form. The piece is in one movement and is divided into four sections by changes of tempo and key. There is no attempt at theme development and little attempt in the exchange of ideas between solo and orchestra. The piano exerts by far the more prominent influence with its virtuosic athletics: extended passage work, octave glissandos, arpeggios, chromaticism, and virtually every effect idiomatic to the keyboard. The work is musically impoverished due to an overbalance of technical gymnastics, though its performance by a capable pianist can hardly fail to make an immediate effect. In keeping with the Romantic concept of uniting the musical and the literary, Weber's *Konzertstück* is programmatic and attempts a musical description of medieval knights, ladies, and crusaders. Program music was a useful aid to Weber and to other Romantic composers who sought new forms to take the place of old ones.

Yet another experiment in the concerto style was achieved by Hector Berlioz (1803-1869). Most notable for his conceptions of expanded orchestral sound and color and for his introduction of the *idée fixe* device, Berlioz envisioned a symphony with viola obbligato which turned out to be a *bona fide* concerto. The work was *Harold in Italy,* composed in 1834 for the legendary Paganini. Contrary to general expectations and to Paganini's wishes as well, the work was not virtuosic in the solo part. It was, in fact, conceived orchestrally and the parts which the tutti and solo play in the customary concerto were reversed, with emphasis on the former rather than the latter. Like the earlier *Symphonie Fantastique, Harold in Italy* is programmatic. Loosely based on Byron's *Childe Harold,* the work is in four movements, the first of which is in sonata form, or Berlioz' version of it. The *idée fixe,* (Example 1), utilized in this work also, serves to unify the lengthy whole with a single fragment of melody.

Example 1.   Berlioz, Harold in Italy.

PAGANINI AND LISZT

Two unrivaled virtuosi of the nineteenth century, Niccolò Paganini (1782-1840) and Franz Liszt (1811-1886), exerted considerable influence on the Romantic concerto. Paganini's feats on the violin are well known and Liszt, who was termed the "Paganini of the piano," was no less proficient at the keyboard. The unheard-of exploits of these two artists caused such a stir that supernatural powers were attributed to them, an explanation which Paganini, in particular, did nothing to refute. Possessing extraordinary skill on their respective instruments, both Paganini and Liszt were more than capable of realizing the resources in each of the instruments. Paganini wrote concertos for the violin (he seldom played anything but his own music), and as he was essentially a virtuoso and master improvisor rather than composer, his scores are merely skeletons of the compositions as he actually performed them. It took the fiery wizardy of Paganini himself to transform the basic elements of a concerto, as sketched on paper, into the fascinating creative experience which musicians and non-musicians alike avowed a performance of Paganini to be. Schubert, Chopin, Liszt, Rossini, and Schumann were all astounded by his ability. Paganini's virtuosity spurred Schumann on as a concert pianist, and he titled one of the episodes in his *Carnaval* after the violinist. Liszt, Brahms, Schumann, and in the twentieth century Rachmaninoff, used the *Caprices* of Paganini as the basis for compositions of their own.

The principal contributions of Liszt in the realm of the concerto are the Piano Concertos in E-flat major and A major and the *Totentanz* for piano and orchestra. All of these works have in common mammoth proportions and overpowering volumes of sound. In the E-flat Concerto, a work really conceived in one movement but sectionalized so as to give the impression of a four-movement plan, Liszt employs theme transformation as a unifying device from section to section. This cyclical device differs from the *idée fixe* of Berlioz in its use of a basic theme throughout the work which is varied in tempo and mood according to its location in the scheme of the composition. The *idée fixe*, a theme which returns throughout the work but remains separate from the rest of the thematic material, does not undergo such modification. In the A major Concerto, Liszt achieves complete continuity of thought in a one-movement concerto, rhapsodic in character, and based on the principle of opposition between solo and orchestra without specific formal design of alternation such as sonata movements have. The *Totentanz* is an early example of theme and variations as a form for solo and orchestra, also used later by Franck (*Symphonic Variations*), Tchaikovsky (*Variations on a Rococo Theme for cello and orchestra*), and Rachmaninoff (*Rhapsody on a Theme of Paganini*).

Though highly virtuosic, the Liszt concertos are nonetheless quite idiomatic to the keyboard. These works rely heavily on their effective pianistic writing but are so loosely constructed that the musical substance itself is imperiled by the lack of concrete design. The orchestra, though it plays a prominent part and is treated in a variety of interesting ways, remains decidedly subordinate to the imperious role of the piano.

Liszt and Paganini, as virtuosos, cast long shadows across the realm of performance practice. Though they contributed much that is musically superficial, they were able to succeed, as no previous instrumentalists had, in elevating the art of solo performance to an unprecedented height. Their fabulous techniques set a new standard of excellence among instrumentalists which affected their contemporaries as well as many generations of musicians to come.

Figure 4. A cartoon of Liszt as a piano-winged hero destroying the dominance of rigid musical forms. Courtesy of The Bettmann Archive.

Piano Concerto No. 1 in E-Flat Major

If competently played, the E-flat Piano Concerto can hardly fail to create a stir, for its pages are brimming with challenges to pianistic technique that will elevate the pianist who can toss them off in grand style to the position of hero in the eyes of most audiences. As though jealous of the orchestra even while conceding the necessity of its presence, Liszt is ever reluctant to share the limelight of his soloist. This work exists for the glorification of the pianist, and all other ideas are held in subordination.

The concerto begins *Allegro maestoso* with a forceful theme in the orchestra, a theme with a tinge of foreboding in its chromatic pattern:

Example 2. Liszt, Piano Concerto No. 1 in E-flat major, First Movement.

The soloist, poised and impatient, is kept waiting only four measures. His entrance, in thundering chords and widely jumping octaves, overshadows at once the initial voice of the orchestra, and, as though to assert further his superiority, the soloist launches immediately into a lengthy and brilliant cadenza which ends with a long trill and a swoop up the keyboard. The orchestra enters again with the opening theme. A quieter, more expressive mood is shortly introduced by the solo clarinet and the piano takes up a new melody:

> **Example 3.** Liszt, Piano Concerto No. 1 in E-flat major, First Movement.

Undercurrents of the original theme begin to intrude on this placid lyricism and finally take over entirely. With renewed vigor the pianist performs long series of octave passages, pausing in a lyrical reminiscence for a brief moment before bringing the movement to a close with harp-like arpeggios.

Muted strings begin the second movement, marked *Quasi Adagio*, but leading later to *Allegretto vivace*. The principal melody, suggested in the opening measures, is almost immediately taken up by the piano:

> **Example 4.** Liszt, Piano Concerto No. 1 in E-flat major, Second Movement.

Two recitative-like passages for the piano follow, culminating in a brief but dramatic cadenza. A long trill by the piano underscores a new melody in the solo flute:

> **Example 5.** Liszt, Piano Concerto No. 1 in E-flat major, Second Movement.

The flute is joined by the clarinet and oboe in repeating the melody, and the music proceeds into the *Allegretto vivace* which is, in effect, a completely new movement.

Designated by Liszt "Capriccioso scherzando," this movement, or section, makes colorful use of the triangle in its score. Contemporary

audiences, accustomed to many varieties of percussion instruments, find
it difficult to imagine the outburst of criticism which greeted this particular part of the concerto when the work was first played. The theme,
in staccato octaves, is heard in the piano after a brief orchestral introduction:

Example 6.   Liszt, Piano Concerto No. 1 in E-flat major, Second
            Movement.

A new theme emerges in the solo flute, with appropriate pianistic
decorations, and the music continues in scherzo fashion until the original
opening theme returns. The mood instantly changes, and the piano again
plunges into the huge chords and skipping octaves which marked the
beginning of the concerto. Presently Example 5 is heard in the oboe,
with the tympani repeating the rhythmic pattern of the first theme. The
movement ends in a blaze of sound in both solo and orchestra.

The now familiar Example 4 opens the third movement, but its
tempo has now changed to *Allegro marziale animato.* Waiting through
an unusually long orchestral tutti, the piano finally comes in with brilliant octaves which terminate in the emergence of Example 5. Repeating
this theme in its original non-martial rhythm, the oboe joins with the
piano, followed by a reappearance of Example 4. While providing the
piano with ample supply of virtuosic material, Liszt now furnishes a
new melody:

Example 7.   Liszt, Piano Concerto No. 1 in E-flat major, Third
            Movement.

This theme is joined by others from the previous movements. Form-
ing the basis for the coda is the original first theme from the opening
movement. In keeping with the spirit of the work, the conclusion is
brilliant and bombastic.

MENDELSSOHN

Composing in a different vein entirely from the bombastic style of
Liszt was Felix Mendelssohn (1809-1847). Mendelssohn, though frankly

sentimental, clothed his Romantic traits in a refinement, a symmetry, and a clarity which approached the Classic ideal. The son of a banker, Mendelssohn was reared with all the advantages of culture and wealth which the social position of the family guaranteed. Well-educated and highly talented, he showed a distinct gift for writing and drawing in addition to his musical prowess. It will be to the eternal credit of Mendelssohn that, at the age of twenty, he arranged and conducted a performance of the *St. Matthew Passion* of the nearly forgotten J. S. Bach. In this single concert, in 1829, Mendelssohn restored an interest in Bach which has endured to this day. A sensitive and dedicated musician, Mendelssohn labored consistently under the highest standards of performance and composition, and his early death deprived musical Europe, too soon, of one of its most promising figures.

Mendelssohn wrote three concertos: Piano Concertos in G minor and D minor and the Violin Concerto in E minor. Sharing the Romantic predilection for minor keys, Mendelssohn made generous use of that modality and frequently demonstrated that the minor mode need not be somber or foreboding. The first piano concerto in G minor is a three-movement work in which the movements are played without a break. Mendelssohn side-steps the issue of the Classical double exposition in the first movement sonata form simply by condensing the material into one exposition rather than two. This is readily accomplished by the immediate introduction of the piano solo. The keyboard writing is rewardingly idiomatic and there are no cadenzas in either of the piano concertos; the orchestration is deftly handled in Mendelssohn's expert manner. The second concerto in D minor, rarely performed today, does not quite attain the level of excellence of the G minor work.

Violin Concerto in E Minor, Op. 64

The Violin Concerto in E minor, Op. 64, remains Mendelssohn's most popular concerto and one of the most beloved of all violin concertos. Completed in September, 1844, it was written for the violinist Ferdinand David, concertmaster of the Gewandhaus Orchestra in Leipzig. The work reveals Mendelssohn's mastery of lyricism and craftsmanship and is unabashedly Romantic in the best sense of the term.

In the first movement, *Allegro molto appassionata,* Mendelssohn again uses his abbreviated version of the Classic first-movement sonata form, writing a single rather than a double exposition. Donald Tovey declares that, with this one stroke, Mendelssohn "destroyed the classical concerto form,"[1] but Mendelssohn's adaptation of the older form still retained structural validity and became the model for many succeeding composers in the concerto realm. Entering after a brief introduction of

one and one-half measures, the solo violin states the principal theme of
the first movement:

Example 8.   Mendelssohn, Violin Concerto, Op. 64, First Movement.

Responding with its own presentation of the same subject, the orchestra
leads into the transition theme:

Example 9.   Mendelssohn, Violin Concerto, Op. 64, First Movement.

The second theme, lyric and tranquil, is introduced by the flutes and
clarinets while the violin has the unusual duty of providing a low pedal-
point on the open G string:

Example 10.   Mendelssohn, Violin Concerto, Op. 64, First Movement.

The transition theme opens the development section in which Mendelssohn again displays a highly individualistic device: the insertion of the
cadenza at the close of the development, leading to the recapitulation.
The orchestra re-enters with the first theme to the accompaniment of
the arpeggios of the concluding cadenza material and the violin continues its role of accompanist until the orchestra is ready to take up
the transition theme once more. The tonality changes to E major for
the second subject which is presented in a fashion similar to its first
entrance in the exposition. The coda proceeds at increased tempo to
the agitated end of the movement.

Linking the first movement to the *Andante* following is a single tied
note in the bassoon—almost imperceptible over the din of the final chords
of the concluding *Allegro* movement. After a brief, quiet interlude, the
solo violin enters with the main theme, now in 6/8 time and in C major:

Example 11.   Mendelssohn, Violin Concerto, Op. 64, Second Movement.

A second, contrasting theme enters before the initial melody returns, completing the ABA form of the movement:

Example 12.   Mendelssohn, Violin Concerto, Op. 64, Second Movement.

Serene and contemplative, the music in this movement makes no pretense at profundity. It is content to portray simplicity and elegance, two attributes which Mendelssohn well knew how to express.

A short but expressive *Allegretto non troppo* functions as the connecting material between the slow and final movements of the concerto. Its theme is given to the solo violin which performs much as a narrator in a continuing tale.

Example 13.   Mendelssohn, Violin Concerto, Op. 64, Third Movement.

The spirited finale, *Allegro molto vivace,* is a rondo in the light, airy character of the scherzo, a mood in which Mendelssohn was never surpassed. The three themes which form the basis for the movement are:

Example 14.   Mendelssohn, Violin Concerto, Op. 64, Third Movement.

Though Mendelssohn's modifications in the structure of the Classic concerto, most notably the use of a single exposition, were made to accommodate his individual ability, his changes followed a constructive rather than a destructive course. His concertos, especially the Violin Concerto, were successful in what they set out to do; his simplification of the first-movement form, far from leading to the devaluation of the concerto, became the prototype for great numbers of concertos since Mendelssohn's time. Although he followed in the footsteps of many of his contemporaries along certain paths, such as the connecting together of movements, Mendelssohn was essentially conservative and his concertos did not follow the highly virtuosic trend evident in many Romantic concertos.

CHOPIN

As the Romantic period witnessed the emergence of the piano as the most popular and prevalent instrument, it also produced Frédéric Chopin (1810-1849) as the composer who understood uniquely the instrument and who wrote perhaps more completely pianistic music than any other person before or since his time. Chopin is the only major composer to write almost exclusively for the piano, and the keyboard literature has been greatly enriched by his compositions. Writing principally short character pieces, Chopin left collections of etudes, preludes, nocturnes, ballades, mazurkas, waltzes, impromptus, polonaises, and scherzos whose popularity has made him a favorite with amateurs and professional musicians for more than one hundred years. While Liszt delighted in huge sizes and sounds, Chopin was a miniaturist by comparison, excelling in those areas where the problems and complications of form are not demanding.

Chopin wrote two concertos for piano and orchestra: the Concerto in E minor, Op. 11, and the F minor Concerto, Op. 21. These, together with the B-flat minor and B minor piano sonatas, represent his major successful works in large forms. By training and by temperament, Chopin was more comfortable when he was working in the intimate and personal style of the short, one-movement piece—the area in which he wrote so prolifically for the piano. The piano concertos, however, are not without merit. In these works Chopin did not attempt to be an innovator but followed more closely than many of his contemporaries the older, established outlines. In each of the concertos there are three movements and these are separated; in each, Chopin uses the orthodox first orchestral tutti in the opening movement which sets forth the main themes prior to the entrance of the solo piano. Once the piano enters, however, it completely dominates the texture of each of the works and subordinates the orchestra to the role of accompanist. Both of Chopin's concertos are youthful works, yet they reveal the mastery of ornamentation and expressiveness for which all of his music is noted.

Though he discovered new tonal colorings and explored the harmonic, chromatic, and rhythmic resources of the piano, Chopin's skill in the field of orchestration was limited. In the concertos, the orchestra supplies only the minimum support for the piano and the orchestration is, on the whole, ineffectual. In the second and third movements of the F minor Concerto there are passages which may be termed exceptional —portions which reveal Chopin in rare examples of excellent orchestration. There have been various attempts to rescore the orchestral parts of the concertos but without success. Inadequate as the orchestration appears to be, efforts to increase the importance and brilliance of the orchestra tend to destroy the delicate balance which Chopin maintained between orchestra and piano.

Even though Chopin's piano concertos are not outstanding examples of the form, they have remained in the repertoire because of Chopin's inimitable pianistic writing, his unsurpassed penchant for melody, and his instinctive aptitude for tone coloring. It is not necessary for Chopin's fame to rest on his concertos; his unique and original contributions to piano literature are more capably exhibited elsewhere.

Piano Concerto in E Minor, Op. 11

Actually the second of the piano concertos in date of composition, the E minor Concerto, Op. 11, was written when Chopin was just twenty years old and still very much in the formative stage of his musical creativity. Shortly after the publication of the two concertos, Chopin turned exclusively to the writing of music for piano solo. His efforts in the realm of solo and orchestra are confined to these early years when he was still probing into various areas in search of the realm where his particular ability was most powerful.

The E minor Concerto opens with a full orchestral tutti in which all the principal themes appear. In many performances, however, most of the opening tutti is deleted, leaving a very short orchestral introduction containing only a statement of the main theme before the piano enters.

Example 15.   Chopin, Piano Concerto in E minor, Op. 11, First Movement.

In bold octaves and chords embellished with arpeggios and rapid passages, the piano sets forth its declaration of the principal theme and proceeds through melodic transitions to the second subject, which appears first in E major:

Example 16.   Chopin, Piano Concerto in E minor, Op. 11, First Movement.

Pages of glittering and decorative passage work in typical Chopinesque pianistic style fill out the remainder of the exposition, adding much in the way of delightful effects but little of real substance.

An orchestral tutti closes the exposition, followed by the piano's entrance with the principal theme in C major signifying the beginning of the development. Consisting mainly of intricate technical display, this section offers little in actual thematic transformation. Chopin relies heavily on the frankly virtuosic, but in the context of the work as a whole, virtuosity does not seem out of place.

A return to the principal theme by the orchestra in the original key marks the appearance of the recapitulation. Similar in most details to the exposition, this section finds the second subject appearing in G major to provide the necessary key contrast. A brilliant coda brings the movement to a close.

The poetic second movement, titled Romance, begins with a short introduction in the muted strings followed by the entrance of the piano. Two themes are presented by the soloist, one in E major and the second in B major:

Example 17.   Chopin, Piano Concerto in E minor, Op. 11, Second Movement.

Making generous use of various devices of ornamentation, Chopin constructs the movement upon these two principal melodies. A brief section in C-sharp minor appears, providing a momentary contrast from the main thematic material. In the final moments the orchestra plays the first subject while the piano indulges in its task of supplying decorative passage work.

A brilliant Rondo follows the slow movement and concludes the concerto. Its rhythmically vital first theme is presented by the piano after a short orchestral introduction:

Example 18.   Chopin, Piano Concerto in E minor, Op. 11, Third Movement.

In decided contrast, the second subject, a plaintive melody over a restless orchestral accompaniment, appears only after the initial thematic material has been extensively explored by both solo and tutti:

Example 19.   Chopin, Piano Concerto in E minor, Op. 11, Third Movement.

When the principal theme re-enters, it appears teasingly in E-flat for eight measures, then slips into its proper key of E major. After another appearance of the secondary theme, a lengthy closing section involving intricate and complicated technical work for the soloist leads ultimately to the close of the movement.

SCHUMANN

For unqualified artistic integrity and consummate Romanticism, the music of Robert Schumann (1810-1856) is unequalled. Exemplifying the finest attributes of the music of his era while displaying few of its weaknesses, Schumann remained consistently faithful to the highest ideals both in his personal and his professional life. Imbued with a natural gift for lyricism and poetic expression, Schumann abstained from the prevalent Romantic temptation to venerate size over substance. Many of his most prominent works, such as the *Carnaval* (Op. 9) and *Kinderszenen* (Op. 15), consist of a series of short pieces—miniatures of design and craftsmanship—in which Schumann's sensitive imagination is expressed intimately and succinctly. Almost without exception his music remains unclouded by the illness which shortened his career and shortly thereafter took his life. Passionate, sentimental, reflective, and often child-like, the music of Robert Schumann is uniquely representative of the Romantic period.

Piano Concerto in A Minor, Op. 54

Though Schumann's success as a composer is frequently associated with his works in shorter forms for the piano and his art songs, he made equally significant contributions in compositions of larger proportions. One of his greatest achievements in any media is the Concerto for Piano and Orchestra in A minor, Op. 54. Begun in 1841, a year following Schumann's marriage to Clara Wieck, the first movement reflects all the enthusiasm, the buoyancy, and the unfailing love and encouragement which remained characteristic of their life together. In its initial form, the opening *Allegro affetuoso* remained for four years as a *Fantasy* in one movement for piano and orchestra. It was not until 1845 that Schumann added two additional movements and realized the work as a concerto. Mme. Schumann gave the first performance of the A minor Concerto in Dresden on December 4, 1845; the first American performance took place in New York at a concert of the Philharmonic Society on March 26, 1859. Since that time the work has remained one of the major concertos in the piano repertoire.

Schumann's penchant for dotted rhythms is evident in the forceful introductory figure in the solo piano which leads to the principal theme, stated first by the orchestra and answered by the piano.

Example 20.   Schumann, Piano Concerto, Op. 54, First Movement.

The bracketed figure (Example 20) is used throughout the movement as a unifying rhythmic-melodic motive. It appears as the second subject, and, after a change in key to A-flat major, it appears in a tender and slow dialogue between piano and orchestra at the beginning of the development section. Following the powerful cadenza, this motive, now in diminution, dominates the coda which brings the movement to a rousing close.

Other themes prominent in this first movement are the transition
theme which occurs following the statements of the principal melody:

Example 21.   Schumann, Piano Concerto, Op. 54, First Movement.

and a variation of this theme which enters at the end of the exposition
section:

Example 22.   Schumann, Piano Concerto, Op. 54, First Movement.

It was not Schumann's intention to pattern this movement after the
Classic concerto although, rhapsodic as the movement is, the general
broad outline of the sonata form is still maintained. Like other Romantic
concertos, this first movement is lacking in an opening tutti and the
solo-orchestra relationship is dominated by the piano. The keyboard
writing is vivid, idiomatic, and effective. Schumann's stylistic characteristics are evident everywhere: in the fiery passages representing
Florestan and the introspective passages depicting Eusebius, the two
imaginary extremes of the composer's personality; in the dramatic dotted-
note rhythms which are Schumannesque clichés; in the long melodic
passages with the theme on top and the accompaniment falling below;
in the rich sonorities of the widely-spaced open chords; in the Bach-
like polyphonic texture; and most significantly, in the fact that Schumann
never writes for mere virtuosic effect.

With the *Intermezzo* movement Schumann employs the fairly common practice of the Romantic concerto composer of using the second
movement as a connecting section between the first and third movements or as an introduction to the *finale*. Short and intimate in style,
this *Intermezzo* is reminiscent of the innocence and simplicity of the
Kinderszenen. In ternary form, the movement opens with a playful dialogue between piano and orchestra:

Example 23.   Schumann, Piano Concerto, Op. 54, Second Movement.

The full-bodied tones of the cellos state the second theme while the piano weaves a florid accompaniment figure above the melody:

Example 24. Schumann, Piano Concerto, Op. 54, Second Movement.

At the end of the coda the music fades to a whisper, a subtle reappearance of the main theme of the first movement enters, leading with a rush of scales into the robust *Allegro vivace*. This movement has an irresistible drive which is almost reckless in its enthusiasm. In sonata form which is actually more "conventional" than that of the first movement, this finale takes as its main theme a subject closely related to the principal theme of the opening movement.

Example 25. Schumann, Piano Concerto, Op. 54, Third Movement.

The second subject with its subtle syncopation, its ignorance of the bar lines, and its duple rhythms within a triple measure, produced particular difficulties for pianists and conductors who first tried to perform this movement!

Example 26. Schumann, Piano Concerto, Op. 54, Third Movement.

The development section presents still another new theme:

Example 27. Schumann, Piano Concerto, Op. 54, Third Movement.

A lengthy coda crowns the movement in a final rush of sound, bringing the concerto to a soaring and masterful close.

In the realm of the concerto, the Romantic era produced no work more truly inspired and magnificently conceived than the Schumann A minor Piano Concerto.* It is fully deserving of its stable place in the present-day concerto repertoire. Dr. Daniel Gregory Mason, composer and writer on music, has this to say of the work:

> The concerto stands as a flawless masterpiece. The themes are inspired. There is no trace of sentimentality or morbidness. The form is ruled by an unerring and fine sense of proportion and line. It is neither too long nor too short. There is no awkwardness, no tentativeness, no striving for effect. No note is unwisely placed. The treatment of both pianoforte and orchestra leaves nothing to be desired, either when the one is set against the other or when both are intimately blended. Though it in no way suggests the virtuoso, it is perfectly suited to the piano, bringing out unfailingly the very best the instrument is capable of.[2]

BRAHMS

At the very height of the Romantic era dramatic modifications of musical styles and techniques were taking place. As the most important composer resisting these changes, Johannes Brahms (1833-1897) championed the forms and the musical objectives found in the works of Mozart and Beethoven. A dedicated Classicist in the midst of a rampant Romanticism, Brahms, in his music, both inherited and transmitted the Classic traditions of an era all but forgotten during his time. While other composers sought to evade the problems posed by Classic patterns, Brahms diligently and almost religiously studied their difficulties and tackled their perplexities. The result of his unremitting efforts was a tremendous revitalization of sonata form, the symphony, and the concerto.

Brahms composed two concertos for piano, one for violin, and a double concerto for violin and cello. Like Beethoven, he struggled over his compositions, often changing them from one medium to another, always subjecting them to the severest self-criticism. A thoughtful, sensitive, and unimpulsive man, Brahms characteristically greeted the diatribes of his detractors with enigmatic silence. Even though his music was not always easily accepted nor popular with audiences accustomed to the ingratiating or purely virtuosic works in great number at the time, Brahms never failed to compose uncompromisingly true to his own inner convictions.

---

*There are additional works by Schumann for solo and orchestra: the *Concertstück* in G major, Op. 92, for piano and orchestra; the Concert-allegro in D minor, Op. 134, also for piano and orchestra; a Cello Concerto in A minor, Op. 129; and a Violin Concerto in D minor. Neither the *Concertstück* nor the Cello Concerto have achieved the popularity of the A minor Piano Concerto.

Piano Concerto No. 1 in D Minor, Op. 15

The last great concerto in the Classic tradition, the Fifth Piano Concerto of Beethoven, was written fifty years before the premiere performance of Brahms' First Concerto in D minor, Op. 15, for piano and orchestra. During the intervening years, various composers had experimented and reshaped the concerto to accommodate the form to new ideas, concepts, and methods of expression. In his First Concerto, Brahms, for the first time in half a century, returned to the old Classic molds and at the same time invested them with a new power of expression on such a gigantic scale that he at once became an unprecedented "Romantic Classicist." The First Concerto is a piece of monumental architectural grandeur. Planned originally as a symphony, it underwent a change to a sonata for two pianos before finally emerging in its present form. The concerto was slow to gain recognition. The austerity of its thematic material, the symphonic quality of the writing, the immense formal scope of the work, and the tremendous demands it makes upon the listener created a formidable barrier between this masterpiece and its first audiences. When Brahms, then only twenty-five, played the concerto for a sophisticated Leipzig audience in January of 1859, it was a complete and dismal failure. Undaunted, the humble young composer wrote to Clara Schumann, "I believe that this is the best thing that could happen to one; it forces one to pull one's thoughts together, and stimulates one's courage. After all, I am only experimenting and feeling may way."[3] In the same Leipzig concert hall in 1895, thirty-six years later, the hall resounded with the enthusiastic roar of the audience as Brahms, now a national hero, conducted while Eugene d'Albert played both of Brahms' piano concertos.

The first movement of the D minor Concerto, *Maestoso,* is reputed to have been influenced directly by the tragic suicide attempt of Schumann, a close and warm friend of Brahms. The entire concerto is closely associated with Brahms' affection for the Schumanns, for Brahms himself considered the second movement, *Adagio,* a musical portrait of Clara. The fateful quality of the music is felt immediately with the rolling timpani and the *fortissimo* basses, over which the strings spell out the principal theme with rugged dynamics:

Example 28.   Brahms, Piano Concerto No. 1 in D minor, Op. 15, First Movement.

The cascading trills and the angular leaps give this unique melody a turbulent and stormy effect. It is significant that the main subject is heard in the key of B-flat instead of the expected D minor, a delaying device used by Beethoven in both the First and Ninth Symphonies as well as in other works. After the tragic first theme has spent its initial vitality, a *cantabile* melody emerges for violins and clarinets:

Example 29.   Brahms, Piano Concerto No. 1 in D minor, Op. 15,
First Movement.

The powerful main theme lashes out again and the opening tutti ends in the tonic major with a closing theme which appears later at the end of the first solo as an important horn motive:

Example 30.   Brahms, Piano Concerto No. 1 in D minor, Op. 15,
First Movement.

Entering simply, without calling undue attention to itself, the piano states a serene theme in D minor, a melody new to the movement:

Example 31.   Brahms, Piano Concerto No. 1 in D minor, Op. 15
First Movement.

Progressing into an impassioned dialogue with the orchestra on the opening theme of the tutti, the piano elaborates also on Example 29 and finds its way into the key of F major and the majestic second subject which the solo presents entirely alone:

Example 32.   Brahms, Piano Concerto No. 1 in D minor, Op. 15,
First Movement.

Beginning with a shower of thundering octaves in the piano, the development section presents the main opening theme, Example 29, and another subordinate theme heard in the opening tutti. At the close of this mighty section, the orchestra and piano come to a *fortissimo* unison on "d." To begin the recapitulation, the piano uses the "d" as the seventh of the E major harmony and presents the main theme in that tonality and then again in A major. Once again the tonic of D minor is delayed as at the beginning of the movement. The second theme appears in this section in the key of D major. A long, extended coda, without a cadenza, brings the movement to a heroic conclusion.

Brahms' piano writing in this concerto, as in the Second Concerto and much of his remaining solo works, is at times fiendishly difficult. It is hardly correct to say that Brahms suppresses virtuosity for it would be difficult to find concertos which make more technical demands upon the performer. They require virtuosity of the highest quality. It is true that Brahms' virtuosity grows out of the material and structure of the work and is not solely ostentatious in concept, but the concertos are virtuosic nevertheless. Brahms' polyrhythms, the characteristic thickness of the chords, his use of unconventional arpeggios, and the wide hand-span necessary for accurate performance have caused pianists from his own day to this to declare his music to be unpianistic and unplayable.

In the tranquil second movement, *Adagio,* the orchestra, like a huge choir, sets forth the main theme, a melody characterized by sweeping phrases of unusual length:

Example 33.   Brahms, Piano Concerto No. 1 in D minor, Op. 15. Second Movement.

The piano enters alone with a chordal treatment of the theme followed by a triplet modification which leads into the second subject:

Example 34.   Brahms, Piano Concerto No. 1 in D minor, Op. 15, Second Movement.

A second theme, heard in the orchestra, alternates with Example 34 to form the middle section of this ternary movement.

Example 35. Brahms, Piano Concerto No. 1 in D minor, Op. 15, Second Movement.

The main theme returns and is followed by a closing section which includes a solo cadenza whose purpose is not surface glitter but sincere expression. The final chords of the movement are punctuated by solemn drum beats.

After the tragedy of the first movement and the solemnity of the second, the dashing, robust rondo completes the concerto with a masterpiece which both contrasts and complements the remainder of the work. The main theme is played first by the soloist alone:

Example 36. Brahms, Piano Concerto No. 1 in D minor, Op. 15, Third Movement.

The second theme, a less bombastic and more expressively melodic one, is also stated by the soloist:

Example 37. Brahms, Piano Concerto No. 1 in D minor, Op. 15, Third Movement.

After the principal subject returns, the key changes to B-flat major where the third main theme is heard in the violins:

Example 38. Brahms, Piano Concerto No. 1 in D minor, Op. 15, Third Movement.

This theme becomes the subject of a fugue which Brahms uses as the development section, changing the key in the meantime to B-flat minor. The recapitulation is followed by a lengthy coda containing two solo cadenzas. The movement ends in a blaze of tonal color with both solo and orchestra exhibiting the full force of their powers.

Violin Concerto in D Major, Op. 77

Twenty years were to elapse before Brahms turned again to the writing of a concerto, this time for violin. Composed for the eminent violinist Joachim, a close and devoted friend of Brahms, the Violin Concerto in D major, Op. 77, was, like the D minor piano concerto which preceded it, slow to gain recognition. Its difficult solo part was considered so clumsy that one critic complained the work was a concerto *against* the violin. Not a performer on the instrument himself, Brahms collaborated closely with Joachim during the composition of the concerto, though the exact extent of Joachim's influence is difficult to assess. He did write the first cadenza, however, for Brahms, in typical Classic tradition and, in recognition of the ability of his friend, had left this section to the discretion of the soloist. Unwilling to risk an extemporaneous cadenza, Joachim composed and later published one which is widely used. Other violinists and composers have also submitted cadenzas for this concerto, so there are several from which to choose.

Brahms approached the Violin Concerto with the same reverence for Classic form that permeated the earlier D minor piano concerto, and, like that work, the Violin Concerto is at once lyric and vigorous, delicate and robust. A tightly knit orchestral tutti outlines all but one of the themes of the first movement, *Allegro non troppo*. The simplicity and serenity in the opening bars belie the tremendous scope of what is soon to follow. The first subject consists of three separate ideas, one following immediately after the other:

Example 39. Brahms, Violin Concerto in D major, Op. 77, First Movement.

Having stated his initial thoughts, Brahms then brings back the first idea, but discards the pastoral aura of the opening appearance, and the theme is given a bold, vigorous character. The second subject follows immediately, it, too, consisting of three distinct parts, but each one of these deriving its material from the first part:

Example 40. Brahms, Violin Concerto in D major, Op. 77, First Movement.

A chordal closing theme, in jagged rhythm, is followed by a slowly rising figure in the woodwinds accompanied by restless strings which culminates in the entrance of the soloist. Flashing across the scene in solitary brilliance, the violin transfigures the opening theme, clothing it in new magnificence. After exchanging vivid phrases with the orchestra, the violin soon quiets into a lengthy series of arpeggios under which can be heard reminiscent bits of the opening subject. Finally the soloist is permitted to exhibit the theme, and for the first time the violin makes the melody truly its own, soaring high above the warm, luscious harmonies of the orchestra. Section "B" of the opening subject returns, invested with richer decorative qualities, followed by a glorified version of section "C." The second subject enters, encompassing the three separate ideas inherent in its thematic material. But when section "C" begins, instead of progressing into the chromatic episode heard in the orchestral tutti, it continues to unfold into a new theme, reserved for the soloist and surpassing in beauty and emotional impact any of the individual subjects presented earlier. As its graceful lines contrast wtih the pizzicato of the orchestra, this delightful and typical Brahmsian melody wends its way into the fabric of the exposition and leaves the listener waiting eagerly for its subsequent return.

Example 41. Brahms, Violin Concerto in D major, Op. 77, First Movement.

Though delayed by the intervention of this new melody, the chromatic portion of section "C" of the secondary theme persists and is finally heard. Not to be forgotten, the arresting closing theme intrudes abruptly, leading relentlessly to the close of the exposition.

In the ensuing orchestral interlude, the strings are given the transformation of the opening theme which marked the solo violin's initial entry. Suddenly Example 41 appears and its fleeting strains are followed again by Example 40-C which the solo also takes up as it enters. Only briefly does the solo violin linger with this familiar material. Leaving the orchestra to continue along the well known path, the solo takes flight in a new melodic counter-melody, a fanciful yet rather melancholy tune which engages the soloist for some span of time:

Example 42.   Brahms, Violin Concerto in D major, Op. 77, First Movement.

As though awakening from a whimsical day-dream, the solo violin abruptly plunges into a series of jolting trills. Immediately the orchestra catches the change of mood and seizes upon the melodic and rhythmic contents of the solo's previous melancholy tune, whipping them into a fierce version of what had previously been gracious and tranquil. Two huge orchestral chords bring this activity to a halt and usher in once again Example 39-C, with the violin striding with giant steps up and down the range of the instrument. Continuing in piercing octaves, the solo plays a version of the closing theme in combination with Example 39-A and brings the brilliant and imaginative development section to a close.

Although the themes in the recapitulation are by now not new, having met them in the exposition and having travelled with them through the dynamic development, the listener is aware of a new, personal meaning in the familiar melodies. They all come forward to make a reacquaintance, and at the proper moment the soloist stands in the spotlight alone for the cadenza.

The closing section following the cadenza is at first complete serenity, with the solo violin reminiscing on the initial first subject. Serenity does not prevail, and the mood of resignation gives way to a flurry of excitement and a rush of double notes in the solo part. In a moment this great concerto movement is finished.

In his original plan for the Violin Concerto, Brahms had included four movements. Always tireless in his self-criticism, the composer found the middle two movements less than satisfactory, removed them, and wrote in their place the present *Adagio*. A movement which is at the same time simple and elegant, the *Adagio* becomes an exquisite song for violin, varied in its tonal color by an extensive use of wind instruments.

Beginning with a choir of woodwinds, the opening melody is set forth in the oboe:

Example 43. Brahms, Violin Concerto in D major, Op. 77, Second Movement.

Only after the winds have completed their picture of the opening melody does the solo violin appear to restate the theme, but not in literal repetition. Brahms uses in this movement an ingenious device of variation in which he expands one measure of the original theme into two measures of variation. Though not readily detected by ear, the technique may be seen by comparing the first few measures of the solo violin part with the theme as presented initially in the oboe:

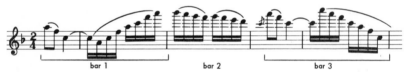

Example 44. Brahms, Violin Concerto in D major, Op. 77, Second Movement.

After pursuing this course for some measures, Brahms turns to the new key of F-sharp minor and contrasting thematic material. Returning in the original key, the principal theme is heard once again in the oboe with the solo violin providing rich accompaniment figures. Climaxing in a passage of theme expansion by the violin over a pizzicato orchestral figure, the music relaxes its intensity and the movement ends quietly.

Turning to a mood of earthy good humor, Brahms provides for the final movement of his Violin Concerto a rondo which remains faithful to the high artistic standards already set in the previous two movements. The solo violin states the opening theme which is almost pianistic in its use of thirds and sixths:

Example 45. Brahms, Violin Concerto in D major, Op. 77, Third Movement.

The orchestra joyfully responds and the tuneful subject is tossed back and forth until a new and even more energetic theme appears in the solo and is immediately inverted by the orchestra:

Example 46. Brahms, Violin Concerto in D major, Op. 77, Third Movement.

After a return of the initial theme, a contrasting section is introduced, shifting unexpectedly from the strong prevailing 2/4 beat to a 3/4 time signature.

Example 47. Brahms, Violin Concerto in D major, Op. 77, Third Movement.

The orchestra tries softly to remind the soloist that he is straying by slipping back into 2/4 time momentarily, but the new melody and its 3/4 beat persist until a series of brilliant scales herald the return of the second subject. Delayed anticipation heightens the effect of the initial theme as it finally reappears with greater enthusiasm than before. A lengthy accompanied cadenza follows, from which both solo and orchestra slip almost unobtrusively into the coda.

Here Brahms uses a technique which strongly characterizes his music: the reorganization of rhythmic stress within the prevailing time signature. Clad in this new guise, the theme frolics with never-waning energy to the conclusion.

In July, 1881, twenty-two years after the completion of his First Concerto, Brahms wrote in typical self-effacing style to a friend: "I don't mind telling you that I have written a tiny, tiny concerto with a tiny, tiny wisp of a scherzo."[4] This "tiny" work, the Concerto in B-flat

Major, Op. 83, for piano, is the *largest* of all concertos in Classic form and is one of the most taxing works in the entire repertoire. Its four movements contain the ultimate achievement of Classic concerto design: they retain the original pliable form as Mozart and Beethoven developed it as well as include the composer's own matchless procedure with the musical materials. The added movement, or the "tiny, tiny wisp of a scherzo," is inserted following the first movement; otherwise the three conventional concerto movements are normal. The piano writing contains Brahms' thick, massive chords, wide leaps, intricate rhythms, and large stretches which are uncompromising in their difficulty. The virtuosity demanded is one of complete technical mastery as well as musical understanding. "It is decidedly not for little girls,"[5] Brahms jokingly remarked to a woman pianist who once performed the work.

Brahms' last concerto, the Concerto for Violin and Violoncello, Op. 102, also suffered at the hands of the critics who found the combination of solo instruments bizarre, the technical difficulties compounded, and the texture unpleasing. With a lesser composer, the results of an endeavor such as the double concerto could have been unrewarding but Brahms' extraordinary skill produced a powerful work from unorthodox instrumentation. Written in three movements, the double concerto is a *tour de force* for the two solo string players, but it is, typically, a work in which the magnitude of Brahms' musical genius outweighs the importance of the technical virtuosity demanded.

OTHER ROMANTIC COMPOSERS

A consideration of the concerto in the Romantic era would not be complete without mention of numerous other composers who contributed to the literature. Space will permit a detailed analysis of just three of these works, but each one is nevertheless completely worthy of study and a sympathetic hearing.

The noted pianist, Anton Rubinstein (1829-1894), wrote five concertos for piano and orchestra which he introduced with considerable success in the concert halls of Europe. Perhaps the best of these is the Concerto No. 4 in D minor, Op. 70. Though the musical substance is somewhat inferior, it is disguised by a brilliant and highly effective solo part.

The music of Peter Tchaikovsky (1840-1893) possesses the ability to make a direct emotional appeal. A student of Rubinstein, Tchaikovsky was instrumental in enhancing the reputation of Russian music in Europe and throughout the world. His Piano Concerto in B-flat Minor, Op. 23, is, without question, one of the best known concertos ever written. Its enormous popularity may be attributed to Tchaikovsky's great skill as a lyricist. His themes tend to be haunting and unforgettable, and, combined with flamboyant pianistic writing, characteristic of many of the Russian concertos, and Tchaikovsky's orchestration, the effect is one of immediate appeal.

Tchaikovsky, Violin Concerto in D Major, Op. 35

Tchaikovsky's Violin Concerto in D major, Op. 35, together with the B-flat minor Piano Concerto, represent his best contributions in the concerto repertoire. Two other works, both in G major for piano, have fallen into obscurity.

Written in the spring of 1878, the Violin Concerto was not performed publicly until late in 1881, and then not by the violinist for whom it was composed, Leopold Auer. In dread of the difficulties presented by the concerto, Auer refused to play it, and the honor of the premiere performance went to Adolf Brodsky, an earlier associate of Tchaikovsky at the Moscow Conservatory. Tchaikovsky was in Switzerland when he wrote the concerto, and its initial performance took place in Vienna where it was only half-heartedly received by the audience and totally condemned by the critics. The most vocal and famous of these, Edward Hanslick, declared that the violin, in Tchaikovsky's concerto, could not be played, only "yanked about . . . torn asunder . . . beaten black and blue."[6] Although Hanslick's opinion of the concerto as a whole was quickly dispelled, the violin part did undergo subsequent revision and simplification, and certain additional changes are still made by performers of the concerto today.

The first movement, *Allegro moderato,* begins with an orchestral introduction which is not so much noted for its presentation of themes as for the expert preparation it gives to the entrance of the soloist. Early in the tutti a pedal point is introduced, creating a short period of suspense which is then relieved by the appearance of the violin with the principal theme.

Example 48.   Tchaikovsky, Violin Concerto in D major, Op. 35,
First Movement.

A transition theme in triplet rhythm is used as the basis for further expansion by both soloist and orchestra, leading into the expressive second subject:

Example 49. Tchaikovsky, Violin Concerto in D major, Op. 35,
First Movement.

This theme is explored thoroughly by solo and orchestra, concluding
with a short closing section at increased tempo, and progressing immediately into the development.

Providing a basis for the beginning of the development section, the
initial theme is used in a martial setting and then changed as it continues, almost giving the effect of an altogether different subject. In
a moment of softened dynamics the orchestra continues with a contrapuntal treatment of new material, based on a two-note phrase motive.
The soloist enters to give a virtuosic description of the second subject.
Again the contrapuntal material is heard, leading to a lengthy and
intricate solo cadenza.

In the recapitulation, the main theme is first heard in the flute
part, but the violin takes charge in the second phrase and this section
continues in a systematic and regular course to the end of the movement. Extensive technical demands are made of the soloist in the spirited
coda.

The original second movement of the Violin Concerto failed to please
Tchaikovsky and he removed it from the context of the work and then
composed, in a single day, the present *Canzonetta*. Embodying the
essence of simplicity, this movement is all the more welcome after the
hustle and virtuosity of the previous *Allegro*. Beginning with a brief
introduction by a choir of wind instruments, the movement contains
two principal themes which are distinctly reminiscent of folk melodies.
Both are presented by the muted solo violin.

Example 50. Tchaikovsky, Violin Concerto in D major, Op. 35,
Second Movement.

There is no full cadence, and the movement actually pauses rather
than ends, leading at once into the vigorous dance-like rondo. It was

this movement which Hanslick described as "brutal, deplorable gaiety" and in which he could envision "savages, vulgar faces . . . coarse oaths."[7]

A short orchestral introduction is followed by the entrance of the soloist in a brief cadenza. The movement then proceeds in predictable rondo fashion, full of verve and brilliance contrasted with expressive eloquence. The first principal theme is initially stated in its entirety by the solo violin following its opening cadenza:

Example 51. Tchaikovsky, Violin Concerto in D major, Op. 35, Third Movement.

Less brilliant, but equally arresting, is the second subject, voiced by the soloist over a drone accompaniment:

Example 52. Tchaikovsky, Violin Concerto in D major, Op. 35, Third Movement.

Presented first as a dialogue between oboe, clarinet, and bassoon, the third theme is heard softly and *molto meno mosso*:

Example 53. Tchaikovsky, Violin Concerto in D major, Op. 35, Third Movement.

A massive coda, signaled by a pedal point in the orchestra, brings the movement to a whirling, sparkling close.

Another Russian composer, Nicolas Rimsky-Korsakov (1844-1908), contributed in a more radical vein to the concerto literature with his Concerto in C-sharp minor, Op. 30, for piano. Written in a one-movement form rather than the conventional three movements used by most Romantic composers including Rubinstein and Tchaikovsky, the work shows the influence of Liszt in its glittering octave passages.

Dvořák, Violoncello Concerto in B Minor, Op. 104

Among the most popular works in the Romantic concerto repertoire is the Violoncello Concerto in B minor, Op. 104, by Antonin Dvořák (1841-1904). Though best known for his "New World" Symphony, Dvořák wrote a great deal of instrumental and chamber music, including the B minor cello concerto and an A minor violin concerto, both of which continue to hold substantial places in the solo concerto realm, and a less successful piano concerto. In an era when musical nationalism was at its height, Dvořák represented his native Czechoslovakia. His music conformed to the trend of the late nineteenth century by drawing from the rich resources of Slavonic folk dance and folk song which were his national heritage. An admirer of Brahms, Dvořák shared a concern for form and organization in his music even as he exhibited those sonorities and rhythms which make his works traditionally Czech.

Of Dvořák's Cello Concerto, Brahms is said to have declared that he had not known it was possible to write a concerto like this. By the time Dvořák began work on this composition, however, his fame as a composer was secure. From his obscure birthplace and his remote homeland he had travelled as far as the United States, not once but twice. The second visit was necessary in order to accept an invitation to be director of the National Conservatory of Music in New York City, a position which Dvořák held for three years from 1892 to 1895. While he was engaged in this endeavor, he wrote, among other works, the Cello Concerto. After returning to his native country, Dvořák found it necessary to make certain changes in the finale, and the work was not performed until 1896.

Displaying a Classical reverence for the opening tutti not always found in nineteenth-century concertos, the first movement begins with an orchestral presentation of the principal themes. The first is heard darkly in the clarinets:

Example 54.   Dvořák, Violoncello Concerto in B minor, Op. 104, First Movement.

Delving only briefly at this time into the possibilities unleashed by this subject, the music proceeds to the second theme, a haunting melody presented here by the horn:

Example 55. Dvořák, Violoncello Concerto in B minor, Op. 104, First Movement.

These two themes form the basis of the movement, though at the close of the tutti a robust, almost raucous, tune appears. Its moment is brief and its purpose of making final preparation for the entrance of the soloist is quickly discharged. Then it is not heard again.

The soloist enters dramatically, fairly spewing out the notes of the principal subject, then retreats into improvisational development of the material. At the proper moment the second subject reappears, this time in the hands of the soloist who treats it with as much care as did the horn earlier.

In the development the once-robust first theme is suddenly, but temporarily, deprived of its vigor. Clothed in a new mantle of pathos, the music here emanates from the deepest recesses of the composer's soul. It is a poignant moment. Woodwinds take up the melody to the accompaniment of a shimmering figure in the cello. The general mood remains quiet until immediately preceding the expected recapitulation. Here the cello streaks upward, but the theme which rushes to meet it is not the first subject, but the second, asserting its right to be here at this moment in a full-bodied statement by the entire orchestra. No argument is possible. Dvořák, in this one stroke, proclaims the validity of his own experimentation with sonata form. Though not an innovator by nature or training, Dvořák tampers with the form which, up to this point, he had strictly observed, and he emerges successful.

The principal subject is eventually heard in the recapitulation, but not until very near the end. There is a short coda which brings the movement to a close, but Dvořák does not include a cadenza.

In the slow movement, *Adagio ma non troppo*, one is transported immediately from the bustle of the metropolis where this work was conceived to the peaceful and idyllic surroundings of Dvořák's native land. Unmistakably the creation of a man who could never feel completely at home far from familiar and beloved soil, this movement reveals the yearning and the bitter-sweet memories of faraway places. The pastoral influence is much in evidence as well as the folk element. With only a little imagination one can envision some of the tunes being played by a group of the itinerant musicians who wandered about the

Czech countryside, stopping at village inns and shops to entertain the populace.

There is an abundance of melodic material in this movement. The main theme is presented first in the woodwinds who then relinquish it to the soloist:

Example 56. Dvořák, Violoncello Concerto in B minor, Op. 104, Second Movement.

More melodies emerge, seemingly growing one out of the other. In the middle section, an effective change of tonality and a bolder theme, reminiscent of a national air, briefly precedes a new and expressive cello melody.

Example 57. Dvořák, Violoncello Concerto in B minor, Op. 104, Second Movement.

The principal theme returns in the horns, and soon the pastoral scene is completed in an accompanied cadenza in which the sounds of field and countryside are clearly discernible.

It is sometimes true that the inspiration which pervades first and second movements of concertos does not find the strength to carry through to the end of the entire work. This concerto must be cited as such an example. The excellence of the first two movements is not found in the third, a rondo. There is ample melodic material, but the music seems to have difficulty in achieving an effect, and its rhythmic drive is constantly interrupted until it seems as though the end will never come into sight. This concerto is not alone in being afflicted with a weak final movement, and, fortunately, this fact has not prevented the work from retaining an immense popularity.

Only the three principal subjects will be outlined here, though there are others which will be obvious even at first hearing. The movement begins in march tempo with an energetic melody in the orchestra which the cello seizes upon at once.

Example 58. Dvořák, Violoncello Concerto in B minor, Op. 104, Third Movement.

A subordinate theme is heard in the cello, beginning hesitantly at first:

Example 59. Dvořák, Violoncello Concerto in B minor, Op. 104, Third Movement.

The third subject, a somewhat undistinguished tune, completes the roster of principal rondo themes:

Example 60. Dvořák, Violoncello Concerto in B minor, Op. 104, Third Movement.

Apparently Dvořák finds it difficult to end this movement, or is reluctant to do so, for the coda stretches on long after it would have appeared appropriate to bring it all to a conclusion. A brief reminder of the principal theme of the first movement greets the ears, and finally the music stirs itself sufficiently to end in the same spirited fashion in which it began.

The nationalist trend of the late nineteenth century produced composers in virtually every country whose music represented a distinct national culture. In Norway, Edvard Grieg (1843-1907) turned to the rich wealth of folk music of his native land and based his prolific compositions on folk tunes and rhythms. A skilled lyricist, Grieg showed little interest in the problems imposed by formal restrictions. His Concerto in A minor, Op. 16, for piano, is notable for its enchanting melodies rather than for its expert form. This concerto, which has enjoyed great popularity, was obviously influenced by the Schumann piano concerto in the same key, though the Grieg work is not as musically sound as the Schumann.

The *Variations Symphoniques* by César Franck (1822-1890) belongs in the same variation category as the Liszt *Totentanz* and the Rachmaninoff *Rhapsody on a Theme of Paganini,* Op. 43. The variation form is an uncommon deviation from the customary sonata structure of most concertos. Consisting of an introduction, six variations, and finale, the Franck concerto is actually one unit, progressing fantasia-like from one section to the next. The entire piece is characterized by the composer's inimitable improvisatory style.

An American composer of the nineteenth century, Edward Mac-Dowell (1861-1908), composed music which failed to exhibit the nationalism of many of his European counterparts. MacDowell received most of his music education in Europe and his compositions reflect the European Romantic tradition. Though he was for a brief time considered America's chief composer, very little of his music is still performed today. MacDowell wrote two piano concertos; the first in A minor is generally regarded as an inferior work. His Concerto No. 2 in D minor, Op. 23, is perhaps MacDowell's best composition.

A man out of step with his time was Sergei Rachmaninoff (1873-1943). One of the most illustrious pianists of the twentieth century and a prolific composer, Rachmaninoff's music is unabashedly Romantic in an age when such a subjective approach is generally disdained. His four piano concertos and Paganini variations for piano and orchestra exhibit the lyric, melancholy, and morbid expressiveness which is typical of the Romantic Russian musical heritage. These works require a performer with virtuoso capabilities. Rachmaninoff's appealing, sentimental melodies have kept his concertos very much in the repertoire.

Rachmaninoff, Rhapsody on a Theme of Paganini, Op. 43

Composed in 1934 and first performed by the composer with the Philadelphia Symphony Orchestra in Baltimore, Rachmaninoff's *Rhapsody on a Theme of Paganini,* Op. 43, has enjoyed continued popularity. A piano concerto in every sense of the word, this work merely substitutes the variation form for the sonata-allegro construction and alignment of movements normally employed. Yielding to an attraction which has allured numerous other composers, Rachmaninoff chose as the basis for this ingratiating composition the last of the 24 Caprices by Paganini. It is rare for a violinist to have influenced piano music to such an extent as did the frantic, nineteenth-century virtuoso, for this particular theme has survived probably more successfully in the keyboard works of Brahms, Liszt, Rachmaninoff and others than in the violin literature.

A brief introduction of eight measures precedes the twenty-four variations which comprise the Rhapsody. In the first variation the composer sketches the harmonic structure of the fascinating theme, while the theme itself follows, inserted between Variations 1 and 2:

Example 61.   Rachmaninoff, Rhapsody on a Theme of Paganini, Op. 43.

Subsequently the variations proceed from one to the next with little perceptible demarcation. For the most part they are brief, offering contrasts in mood and technique.

An unusual companion to the sparkling Paganini theme makes an appearance in Variation 7, again in Variation 10, and in the final Variation. Here Rachmaninoff inserts the ominous *Dies Irae*, a part of the Catholic Requiem Mass for the Dead.

Example 62.   Rachmaninoff, Rhapsody on a Theme of Paganini, Op. 43.

The gloomy effect of this ancient melody was bound to attract the melancholy side of Rachmaninoff's personality. Having used the *Dies Irae* in a previous composition (*The Isle of the Dead*), Rachmaninoff skillfully mingles it into the fabric of the Rhapsody. Later, as if enchanted by this foreboding tune, he incorporates it again into his Third Symphony and the Symphonic Dances.

With the eleventh Variation there is a change from an energetic to a tranquil mood, but the transformation encompasses only Variations 11 and 12 (the lovely *Tempo di Menuetto*) before the theme, with renewed vigor, bursts again upon the scene. Variation 16 begins another quiet interlude, culminating in the highly lyric and deeply romantic Variation 18, whose melody is nothing more than a cleverly turned inversion of the Paganini theme. The spell of this entrancing music is broken by an abrupt pizzicato variation, begun by the strings and continued with equal effectiveness in the piano. This variation would surely have delighted Paganini, for its rapid tempo and widely spaced leaps provide marvelous opportunity for the display of dexterity and unerring marksmanship.

With continued rapid tempo, the music builds in intensity. Rhythmic ingenuity is heard in Variation 21 as the piano plays *un poco piu vivo*.

Rachmaninoff's Russian temperament is evident in darkly ominous Variation 22, and as the music progresses to the final variation the *Dies Irae* resounds one last time from the full orchestra. After all the pomp and commotion, the composition ends softly, with a tongue-in-cheek shrug of the shoulders, contradicting the formidable difficulties both soloist and orchestra have been required to conquer before attaining the finish.

A most gratifying feature of Rachmaninoff's music is the fact that much of it is available on records with the composer himself as piano soloist. These reproductions sacrifice little of the high fidelity demanded by current standards and they offer much that is invaluable in the interpretation and sheer piano mastery of this great composer.

Many of the nineteenth-century composers of concertos were faced early in the century with the problem of fitting Romantic ideas into the strict Classic form found in Mozart and Beethoven. The struggle with the problem of the sonata form of the first movement led to connecting movements and even to the one movement concerto. Weber and Berlioz resorted to quasi-programmatic concertos as an aid to problems of form. Other more conservative composers adhered more closely to Classic structure but with certain modification: Mendelssohn reduced the Classic double exposition to a single exposition; Chopin, Schumann, and Brahms managed to infuse Romanticism in the form without radical destruction of Classic ideals.

The piano continued to be the main solo instrument. A fuller realization of the possibilities of the instrument was explored particularly by Liszt; his counterpart of the violin, Paganini, pushed the capabilities of the violin to the same extremes. The solo parts, performed by great virtuoso artists, completely dominated the orchestra in most Romantic concertos though the orchestra developed more and more into a virtuoso performer itself, and, late in the century, the increasing importance of the orchestra became most apparent in the concertos of Brahms.

BASIC LISTENING:

LISZT, Piano Concerto No. 1 in E-flat major
MENDELSSOHN, Violin Concerto in E minor, Op. 64
CHOPIN, Piano Concerto in E minor, Op. 11
SCHUMANN, Piano Concerto in A minor, Op. 54
BRAHMS, Piano Concerto No. 1 in D minor, Op. 15
———, Violin Concerto in D major, Op. 77
TCHAIKOVSKY, Violin Concerto in D major, Op. 35
DVOŘÁK, Violoncello Concerto in B minor, Op. 104
RACHMANINOFF, Rhapsody on a Theme of Paganini, Op. 43

ADDITIONAL SUGGESTED LISTENING:

WEBER, Konzertstück in F minor
BERLIOZ, Harold in Italy
LISZT, Piano Concerto in A major
MENDELSSOHN, Piano Concerto in G minor
CHOPIN, Piano Concerto in F minor, Op. 21
BRAHMS, Piano Concerto No. 2 in B-flat major, Op. 83
————, Concerto for Violin and Violoncello, Op. 102
TCHAIKOVSKY, Piano Concerto in B-flat minor, Op. 23
GREIG, Piano Concerto in A minor, Op. 16
FRANCK, Variations Symphoniques
RACHMANINOFF, Piano Concerto No. 3 in D minor, Op. 30

ADDITIONAL READING:

VEINUS, ABRAHAM, *The Concerto.* New York: Doubleday, Doran and Company, Inc., 1944. Chapter VI.

FOOTNOTES

[1] Donald F. Tovey, *Essays in Musical Analysis,* Volume III, Concertos, London: Oxford University Press, 1937, p. 178.

[2] Edwin John Stringham, *Listening to Music Creatively.* (Englewood Cliffs, N. J.: Prentice-Hall, Inc., 1959), p. 466, citing Leland Hall (Ed. in charge), *The Art of Music.* 14 vols. (New York: National Society of Music, 1915). VII, 237.

[3] Daryl Dayton, "The Piano Concertos of Brahms," Symphony Magazine, Los Angeles Philharmonic Orchestra, Thirty-fourth Season, 1952-1953, p. 22.

[4] *Ibid.,* p. 29.

[5] Walter Niemann, *Brahms,* translated by Catherine Alison Phillips (New York: Alfred A. Knopf, 1949), p. 319.

[6] Julian Herbage, "Peter Ilich Tchaikovsky (1840-1893)," *The Concerto,* edited by Ralph Hill (Baltimore: Penguin Books, 1952), p. 219.

[7] Richard Anthony Leonard, *A History of Russian Music* (New York: The Macmillan Company, 1957), p. 188.

chapter 6

the twentieth-century concerto

Twentieth-century composers, in violent reaction to the music of Wagner, German Romanticism, and the extravagancies of nineteenth-century program music, have frequently sought refuge in the standard forms of previous centuries. New interest and inspiration have been found in such abstract forms as the symphony, the sonata, and, of course, the concerto. Ernest Bloch, Igor Stravinsky, and Paul Hindemith are three composers who have written concerti grossi after the manner of the older Baroque form. The return to older forms is an important feature of Neoclassicism, and many of the finest twentieth-century concertos may be termed "Neoclassic." There is considerable freedom in the new use of the older concerto forms and, in addition, the basic elements of music have undergone great change. New concepts in melody, harmony, and rhythm are particularly striking.

If any generality may be made concerning twentieth-century concertos, it is that the orchestra is elevated to an equal plane with the soloist. In most nineteenth-century concertos, particularly in Romantic piano concertos, the soloist is all important and frequently overbalances the orchestra. The modern orchestra, however, is itself a virtuoso instrument; players and instruments have reached a stage of perfection unheard-of in earlier times. The conductor has replaced the soloist as chief virtuoso. So it is not surprising to find a contemporary composer such as Bartók writing a concerto for *orchestra*—a demanding work feasible only in a period of great orchestral technical proficiency.

RAVEL

Though principally Impressionistic, the works of Maurice Ravel (1875-1937) reveal other characteristics as well. There is an attentiveness to formal clarity in his music that gives it a Neoclassic quality. Ravel's String Quartet, the Sonatine for piano, and his last two major compositions, the Piano Concerto in G major and the Concerto for Left Hand, are pertinent examples of his affinity for Classic forms. When Ravel visited the United States on a concert tour in 1928, he became interested in the jazz styles flourishing at that time, and he later incorporated touches of American jazz into both of his concertos.

Piano Concerto in G Major

Ravel wrote his Piano Concerto in G major at the request of the Boston Symphony Orchestra who wished the composer to appear as soloist in the first performance of the work during the anniversary of the orchestra's fiftieth season. Unfortunately, the plans were not entirely realized, for the composition of the concerto occupied Ravel much longer than he had anticipated and, due to ill health, he was unable to make the return trip to the United States. In January of 1932, the concerto finally received its premiere performance in France.

In three movements, the G major Concerto adheres closely to Classic formal models. The first and last movements are technically demanding for the soloist; the second movement is a contrasting melodic *Adagio*. Characterized by strong rhythmic patterns, the G major Concerto reveals the composer veering away from pure Impressionism toward a clarity of texture more closely associated with Neoclassicism.

If any adjective could be chosen to describe the G major Concerto as a whole, "exuberant" would seem to be most applicable. The work abounds in effusive good spirits, in a spontaneous expression which gives no indication of contrivance. Its first movement, *Allegramente*, opens with both piano and orchestra participating, but the principal theme is given to the piccolo, then to the trumpet. The mood is one of unrestrained gaiety such as might be found at one of the village festivals in the Basque country, where, in fact, Ravel was born.

Example 1.   Ravel, Piano Concerto in G major, First Movement.

Permission for reprint granted by Durand et Cie., Paris—Copyright Owner
Elkan-Vogel Co., Inc., Philadelphia—Sole Agent.

The festivity reaches a climax, then subsides, and a transitional theme appears in the piano, a languid melody that brings with it a hint of Spain:

Example 2.   Ravel, Piano Concerto in G major, First Movement.

As though lifting the spirits from some low ebb to an unbelievable height, the secondary theme appears in the piano, rising slowly but firmly to its peak. This extremely effective melody is punctuated by soft stabs of dissonant chords.

Example 3.   Ravel, Piano Concerto in G major, First Movement.

After the orchestra has taken a turn at expressing the theme, the tempo reverts to the whirling, toccata-like pace of the opening measures. Assuming the place usually occupied by the development, this section, though shorter than most conventional developments, culminates in the recapitulation of the principal theme in the piano part.

The languid transition theme returns, varied by a bit of ornamentation. There follows immediately an ethereal cadenza for harp, based on a section of the previous theme. Interrupted rudely by a sudden intrusion of the soloist and orchestra making unconventional sounds, the cadenza continues, divided now among several instruments: bassoon, flute, clarinet, and oboe.

Appearing immediately in the form of a piano cadenza, the secondary theme, with greater tonal color and embellished by long series of trills, makes it final entrance. Joined ultimately by the orchestra, the piano gives an inspiring declamation of this eloquent melody before embarking into the rapidly paced closing section. It is perpetual motion until the conclusion of the movement, with the final chords being based on an Oriental modal scale.

Contrasting in tempo and general mood, yet retaining a spirit of spontaneous vitality, the second movement, *Adagio assai,* begins with a long piano solo in which the right hand melody is accompanied by a chaconne-like bass, a figure which persists in each measure throughout this movement.

Example 4. Ravel, Piano Concerto in G major, Second Movement.

Permission for reprint granted by Durand et Cie., Paris—Copyright Owner Elkan-Vogel Co., Inc., Philadelphia—Sole Agent.

Just when it seems certain that the entire *Adagio* will belong to the piano alone, the orchestra joins and remains in association with the soloist until the finish. Individual woodwind instruments have special importance in this movement, various of them being given solo parts while the piano weaves arabesque figurations to enhance the melody. The opening theme is heard at the beginning and again at the close, while other melodic material occupies the intervening pages.

The third and final movement, *Presto,* has all the characteristics of a perpetual motion. Not a moment of relaxation is offered soloist or orchestra as the music plummets across the scene with a dazzling array of colors. Jazz effects, snarling trombones, biting woodwinds, even a whiplash, plus a piano part filled with intricate cross-hand technique and glittering finger passages create a mood of breathless activity. The principal theme is quoted here in its simplest form, deprived of the ornamental notes which surround it:

Example 5. Ravel, Piano Concerto in G major, Third Movement.

Permission for reprint granted by Durand et Cie.. Paris—Copyright Owner Elkan-Vogel Co., Inc., Philadelphia—Sole Agent.

A fitting and highly successful climax to this "exuberant" concerto, the finale concludes with a drum roll and the whirl of a tambourine.

The Concerto for Left Hand, on which Ravel was working simultaneously with the G major Concerto, was composed for a well-known Austrian pianist who had lost his right arm during World War I. Accepting the limitations as a challenge, Ravel wrote a work rich in imagination, vitality, and expressive power. Conceived in a one-movement scheme with three sections, the concerto is, in mood and construction, much less conventional than the G major Concerto. The performance makes tremendous demands upon the soloist, who must, with one hand, achieve technical and musical effects ordinarily requiring two hands. Widely acclaimed and frequently performed, the Concerto for Left Hand is Ravel's final major composition. An automobile accident in 1932 caused a breakdown in his health from which he was never able to recover, though his death did not occur until 1937.

BARTÓK

Acknowledged now as one of the major composers of this age, Béla Bartók (1881-1945) unhappily never succeeded in winning a secure reputation for his music during his lifetime. It is only since his death that his superlative work has gained general recognition. Shunned and rebuked, Bartók was driven into the conditions of poverty and ill health generally associated only with artistic personalities of centuries ago. Composing with undiluted power until his death, Bartók achieved a delicate balance between the folk elements of his native Hungary and the distinguishing traits of harmony, rhythm, and structure which make his style unique. Aware of the direction in which Hungary was being drawn in the politically turbulent days of 1940, Bartók fled his native land and came to the United States. His reception here was not cordial and efforts to obtain a permanent position which would offer him financial support were fruitless. Bereft of funds and deprived of musical recognition, Bartók's death from leukemia and malnutrition completes a tragic picture.

In the realm of the concerto Bartók made significant contributions. His best known work in the literature is the Concerto for Orchestra, a composition in five movements, less esoteric and more easily accepted than many of Bartók's other works. There are, in addition, three piano concertos, a viola concerto, and two concertos for violin.

Violin Concerto No. 2

The Violin Concerto No. 2 is one of Bartók's outstanding works in large form. Structurally, the work is patterned after Classic principles;

the first and last movements are in sonata form with the second movement a theme and variation. The Concerto is permeated with Hungarian folk music which Bartók, very early in his career, had assimilated into his own personal style. The solo part gives remarkable evidence of a full understanding of the technical and tonal possibilities of the instrument. Complicated rapid passages, wide leaps, arpeggiated figures, and trills alternate with slower, melodic sections of tremendous expressive power.

The first movement, *Allegro non troppo*, begins with soft, repeated chords on the harp which introduce the soloist and the principal theme:

Example 6.   Bartók, Violin Concerto No. 2, First Movement.

A subsidiary melody, in faster tempo, follows the violin's initial statement of the principal theme:

Example 7.   Bartók, Violin Concerto No. 2, First Movement.

The solo part builds with accumulative energy to a restatement of the main subject by the full orchestra. Preparing for the second subject, the violin engages in the repetition and development of this short motive fragment:

Example 8.   Bartók, Violin Concerto No. 2, First Movement.

Just prior to the appearance of the second subject, harp glissandos can be heard, followed by the entrance of the violin, at a reduced tempo, in the statement of the secondary subject:

Example 9. Bartók, Violin Concerto No. 2, First Movement.

The development section begins *vivace* in the solo part. There are sharp, syncopated orchestral chords contrasted with rapid passage work in the violin. Double stops add to the complexity of the soloist's performance. In one section of the development, the violin plays an inversion of the principal theme to an accompaniment of harp and celesta arpeggios and an undercurrent of strings. The recapitulation begins without the harp chords heard at the beginning and proceeds regularly, though more compactly than the exposition, to the end. A long and intricate solo cadenza, written into the score by the composer, precedes the lengthy, vigorous coda.

The second movement, *Andante tranquillo,* is a theme and six variations. Poignantly reminiscent of peasant folk tunes, the theme is stated by the violin over a soft, orchestral accompaniment:

Example 10. Bartók, Violin Concerto No. 2, Second Movement.

Improvisational in character, the first variation recalls the nomadic Gypsy string players of Bartók's native country. The solo violin gives the illusion of a melody half played and half spoken. A lyric treatment characterizes the second variation, with special emphasis given to the ornamental harp part. The third variation is sharply rhythmic, with harsh dissonances and changing meters. Featuring decorative material and an abundance of trills in the solo part, the fourth variation concludes with a short canon between the solo violin and the strings of the orchestra. The fifth variation is strongly rhythmic and in the character of a scherzo. Returning to the contrapuntal vein, the last variation is again a canon, with the violin offering color in the form of trills, repeated notes, and runs. To close the movement, the original, plaintive theme is repeated.

In the final movement, *Allegro molto,* Bartók's fondness for a powerful, vigorous rhythmic drive is evident and is closely related to the "primitive" rhythmic stress of his early compositions. Filled with savage repeated-note figures, whirling passage work, excruciatingly difficult double notes and octaves, and laced throughout with intricate contrapuntal writing, the music relents only occasionally to permit lyric passages. The violin at times closely approximates the percussive tone quality of the piano. After a brief orchestral introduction, the solo states the main theme alone:

Example 11. Bartók, Violin Concerto No. 2, Third Movement.

Copyright 1941 Hawkes & Son (London) Ltd. Reprinted by permission.

Many of the themes in the finale have a close melodic relationship to those in the first movement. Typical of this relationship is the secondary theme which bears striking resemblance to the principal theme of the first movement (See Example 6).

Example 12. Bartók, Violin Concerto No. 2, Third Movement.

Copyright 1941 Hawkes & Son (London) Ltd. Reprinted by permission.

A complex development and compressed recapitulation are followed by a coda in which Bartók utilizes exotic color effects in the orchestra. Requiring a large ensemble, the instrumentation for the Violin Concerto includes two flutes, two oboes, piccolo, English horn, two clarinets, bass clarinet, two bassoons, contra bassoon, four horns, two trumpets, two tenor trombones, bass trombone, timpani, two side drums, bass drum, two cymbals, triangle, tam tam, celesta, harp, and strings.

SCHOENBERG, BERG, STRAVINSKY, AND HINDEMITH

A composer whose music has come to be associated almost entirely with the twelve-tone system which he formulated, Arnold Schoenberg (1874-1951) created a distinct musical vocabulary and devised a different system of working with familiar material that has exerted wide influence on the art of composition in this century. Writing in many forms and media, Schoenberg has been credited with the destruction of traditional harmonic and melodic conceptions and the resultant atonality. At first viewed as extremely radical and inaccessible, Schoenberg's music has now gained acceptance and his methods have been followed by many major contemporary composers. Among Schoenberg's concertos are the Piano Concerto (1942) and the Violin Concerto (1936) which both employ the twelve-tone, or serial technique.

A pupil and friend of Schoenberg, Alban Berg (1885-1935) followed, in theory, the formulas of construction devised by his teacher, but Berg's music is more nearly a compromise between the twelve-tone, atonal method and traditional tonal and harmonic patterns. As a result, his work lacks the stark, lean quality characteristic of much twelve-tone music. Berg's opera, *Wozzeck*, contains writing that is warmly Romantic, and this trend is evident in his other scores as well.

Berg is represented in the concerto form by two compositions: the Chamber Concerto for Violin, Piano and Thirteen Wind Instruments (1925) and the Violin Concerto (1935). Composed on the occasion of Schoenberg's fiftieth birthday, the Chamber Concerto is an atonal composition whose formal structure is based on the number "3" and its multiples. There are instrumental groups (keyboard, strings, winds), musical themes devised from the three names of Schoenberg, Berg, and Webern, and other symbolism based on the same numerology. The Violin Concerto, Berg's last completed work, was written for the American violinist Louis Krasner. The composer did not live to hear the premier of the Concerto which occurred during the following year. Written in two movements, the Violin Concerto fuses the twelve-tone system with more traditional tonal relationships to create a style Romantic though atonal, similar to the effect achieved in *Wozzeck*. In the first movement can be heard popular tunes; in the second movement, in striking contrast to Berg's twentieth-century style of writing, there suddenly appears the chorale "Es ist genug" found in J. S. Bach's cantata *O Ewigkeit du Donnerwort*. Berg's use of the Bach harmonies beside his own gives rise to startling comparisons in the styles of the two musical periods.

Towering above many of his contemporaries as one of the most influential musical personalities of the twentieth century, Igor Stravinsky (1882-   ) is a performer, prolific composer, and conductor of rare vitality. His works exhibit a variety of styles, from the lush *Fire Bird* to the concertos for various instruments which display the purity of the composer's unadorned Neoclassic writing. Composing for such instruments as the piano, violin, and horn, Stravinsky concertos have in common an economy of material and a percussive rather than lyric use of the piano.

A composer whose style is Neoclassic, Paul Hindemith (1895-1963) writes music which is dissonant but tonal albeit not tonal in the conventional major-minor concept of the term. Hindemith did not attempt to abolish tonal centers but rather he created a unique tonal system of his own. In his *The Craft of Musical Composition*, a two-volume text, the theoretical essence of his system is explained. The rules of the method are so logical and so regular that it is not difficult to imitate the Hindemith style.

A most prolific composer, Hindemith wrote in nearly every form and for all instruments. Between 1947 and 1949 he composed a series of concertos for wind instruments. His Clarinet Concerto (1947) was dedicated to Benny Goodman and was first performed by him in Philadelphia in 1950. Other concertos in this series include the Horn Concerto (1949), the Concerto for Trumpet, Bassoon and Orchestra (1949), and a Concerto for Wood-wind, Harp and Orchestra (1949). An accomplished violist, Hindemith left two concertos for that instrument: *Der Schwanendreher* for Viola and Small Orchestra (1935) and *Trauermusik* for Viola and Strings (1936). Also important are the Violin Concerto (1939), the Cello Concerto (1940), and the Piano Concerto (1945).

Not only a gifted composer but also a dedicated teacher, Hindemith was able to express his musical ideas in compositions and in literary writings as well. Consequently, his influence on contemporary music has been widespread and powerful.

PROKOFIEV

Nicolas Slonimsky cited the music of Serge Prokofiev (1891-1953) as "probably the greatest single influence in Soviet music."[1] A precocious musician in the Mozartean sense, Prokofiev improvised at five years of age, composed piano pieces at six, and wrote an opera (for voices and piano) at nine. His formal study of music began at age eleven when he became a student of Reinhold Gliere, and by the time he entered the St. Petersburg Conservatory in 1904 at thirteen years of age, he had many compositions to his credit. The formidable list included four operas, two sonatas, a symphony, and a large number of piano pieces. Prokofiev remained at the Conservatory for ten years, studying with Glazunov, Liadov, Rimsky-Korsakov, Tcherepnin, and Annette Essipova. Possessed of a daring spirit which readily became evident in his music, Prokofiev earned the reputation of an incorrigible personality with radical musical ideas. His early compositions shocked not only his audiences but his professors at the Conservatory as well, but his outstanding work won for him highest honors upon graduation and for his performance of the First Piano Concerto he was awarded a grand piano.

Prokofiev's favorite medium was always the piano. As a young child he heard his mother, a talented pianist, playing the standard works, and Prokofiev himself became a brilliant concert virtuoso. His five piano concertos reveal the essence of his keyboard style: a percussive use of the instrument tempered with an understanding of its lyric, melodic possibilities. In addition to the piano concertos, Prokofiev wrote two violin concertos, the second, in G minor, having achieved special popularity. Prokofiev was not a radical innovator nor did he devote himself to the surge of musical forces which were causing such a stir in other musical circles. His music, though dissonant, is always tonal; though often satirical, it has moments of lyric Romanticism, yet it definitely leans toward Classic orderliness. The thundering and percussive *style mécanique*, Prokofiev's trademark at the keyboard, never completely overshadows his gift for lyric expression.

Piano Concerto No. 3 in C Major

The Third Piano Concerto in C major has become the most popular of Prokofiev's concertos for keyboard. Occupying the composer for a period of four years, the work was completed in 1921. The first performance was in Chicago on December 16 of that year with Prokofiev as soloist and Frederick Stock as conductor of the Chicago Symphony Orchestra. Critics were divided in their opinions of the Concerto and the work made its way only slowly to its present position of eminence among modern concertos. Bursting with exuberance and vitality, the Concerto's clarity of structure and thematic material make fewer intellectual demands upon the listener than do many concertos in the contemporary idiom.

The first movement begins with a slow introduction by the orchestra with the clarinet voicing the introductory theme:

Example 13.   Prokofiev, Piano Concerto No. 3, First Movement.

Gradually the music increases in speed and force until the orchestra is joined by the solo piano for its statement of the principal theme:

Example 14. Prokofiev, Piano Concerto No. 3, First Movement.

Widely spaced unison passages achieve a crisp tonal effect in the keyboard part; contrasting sections of massive, dissonant chords create a battery of tone clusters. The second theme, given to the orchestra, is a saucy, sarcastic melody heard first in the oboe, then repeated by the piano:

Example 15. Prokofiev, Piano Concerto No. 3, First Movement.

The development section begins with an expressive orchestral statement of the introductory theme (Example 13) to which the piano also lends its voice. An extremely effective return to the recapitulation is achieved by toccata-like piano passages over *pizzicato* orchestral chords. A relentless rhythmic propulsion leads to the climax as the main theme reappears. The return of the second theme is marked by a series of piano glissandos, and the coda again makes use of the rapid passage work which precedes each entry of the main theme.

The second movement, a theme with five variations, is based on an unaffected, march-like melody heard initially in the flutes and clarinets:

Example 16. Prokofiev, Piano Concerto No. 3, Second Movement.

The variations which follow exhibit a wide variety of moods and methods of expression, from lush, chromatic chords to grotesque, brittle figures. Prokofiev's expert orchestration adds to the effectiveness of this movement.

Returning with renewed vigor to the bombastic style of the first movement, the finale is a *tour de force* of pianistic effects, abounding in tortuous gyrations, crashing sonorities, and sparkling glissandos. The opening theme is heard first in the bassoon, accompanied by *pizzicato* strings:

Example 17.   Prokofiev, Piano Concerto No. 3, Third Movement.

Copyright by Edition Gutheil. Copyright assigned to Boosey and Hawkes, Inc. 1947. Reprinted by permission.

Arising from the midst of all the speed and clatter is a contrasting middle section with a Romantic melody:

Example 18.   Prokofiev, Piano Concerto No. 3, Third Movement.

Copyright by Edition Gutheil. Copyright assigned to Boosey and Hawkes, Inc. 1947. Reprinted by permission.

Developing this theme to the fullest, the piano and orchestra then turn with refreshed furor to the reappearance of the principal subject. Heaping one brilliant effect upon another, tension accumulates until the final relief of the last tremendous chords.

Though the music of Prokofiev sounds almost traditional in comparison with the work of twelve-tone composers, it is nevertheless not without contemporary intellectual validity. His music has a wide appeal and has created for Prokofiev a respected place among twentieth-century musicians.

BARBER

Numbering among the most prominent American composers of the twentieth century, Samuel Barber (1910-   ) has earned a secure reputation both here and in Europe. Though best known for his two early works *Adagio for String Orchestra* (1936) and the *Essay for Orchestra* (1938), Barber has made significant contributions in many other areas of composition. His Piano Sonata, Op. 26 (1949), the setting of Matthew Arnold's poem *Dover Beach,* Op. 3 (1931), the Violin Concerto, Op. 14 (1939), the cantata *Prayers of Kierkegaard,* Op. 30 (1954), and the opera *Vanessa* (1958) are a few of his most representative works.

Piano Concerto, Op. 38

Among Barber's recent compositions is the Piano Concerto, Op. 38, already acclaimed as one of the most important works of its kind in the last quarter of a century. Commissioned by the G. Schirmer publishing company in commemoration of the 100th anniversary of the firm, the Concerto was first performed in New York on September 24, 1962, as part of the ceremonies celebrating the opening of the Lincoln Center for the Performing Arts. The soloist on this occasion was John Browning who appeared with the Boston Symphony Orchestra under the direction of Erich Leinsdorf. In 1963 Samuel Barber was awarded the Pulitzer Prize for the Concerto.

The Piano Concerto follows the traditional three-movement pattern. Opening the first movement, *Allegro appassionato,* the piano states an introductory theme *quasi recitativo*:

Example 19.   Barber, Piano Concerto, Op. 38, First Movement.

Copyright 1962 by G. Schirmer, Inc. Used by permission.

The orchestra, with sharp chords, punctuates the soloist's declamation and continues with the unfolding of the principal theme:

Example 20.   Barber, Piano Concerto, Op. 38, First Movement.

Copyright 1962 by G. Schirmer, Inc. Used by permission.

The recitative theme is again heard in a transition before the orchestra, in slower tempo, states the secondary subject:

Example 21.   Barber, Piano Concerto, Op. 38, First Movement.

Copyright 1962 by G. Schirmer, Inc. Used by permission.

A tightly woven movement, the *Allegro* has an added unifying device: the close thematic relation of its melodies. The three principal themes have obvious structural similarities, the interval of a sixth being especially prominent in each.

During the development the rhythmic figures and theme heard in the introductory recitative are predominant. In a quiet orchestral interlude near the end of this section, the theme is inverted. A lengthy solo cadenza appears at the close of the development, a cadenza written out by the composer and intended as an integral part of the score. Based principally on a further expansion of the main theme, the cadenza is highly virtuosic, with intricate chordal, octave, and chromatic passages.

The end of the cadenza marks the reappearance of the main subject in the orchestra and the beginning of the recapitulation. Occurring again as a transition theme, the recitative melody is here inverted. When the second theme appeared earlier in the exposition, it was stated by the orchestra and never by the solo piano. However, in the recapitulation the piano introduces the second theme with the orchestra providing an accompaniment over a long pedal point. The recitative theme creeps in again and, in combination with the principal theme, becomes the basis for the short but effective coda.

In mood and style, many of Barber's works may be termed "Neoromantic." A case in point is the second movement *Canzone*. Melodious and hauntingly beautiful, this movement is mono-thematic; all material throughout is based on one main theme. The theme itself grows out of the accompaniment figure which begins half a measure before the melody enters. Heard in dialogue between flute and oboe, the theme is first stated by the orchestra. Barber introduces a wide variety of tonal coloring in the different appearances of the enchanting melody.

Example 22. Barber, Piano Concerto, Op. 38, Second Movement.

The final movement, *Allegro molto*, is based on the *ostinato* principle, or the repeated and regular reoccurrence of a melodic figure throughout the composition. In rondo form, the movement has a time

signature of 5/8 which the composer indicates must be performed in
accent groups of two plus three in the opening section, three plus two
in the middle part, and back to the two plus three emphasis in the
last section.

Preceded by a short introduction of biting chords in the orchestra
the piano plays first the ostinato figure in the bass:

Example 23.   Barber, Piano Concerto, Op. 38, Third Movement.

Copyright 1962 by G. Schirmer, Inc. Used by permission.

While the left hand continues with the ostinato bass, the right hand
presents a highly rhythmic and melodically dissonant figure which leaps
over a wide range of the keyboard:

Example 24.   Barber, Piano Concerto, Op. 38, Third Movement.

Copyright 1962 by G. Schirmer, Inc. Used by permission.

Later, the orchestra relieves the soloist of the ostinato figure for a short
time to enable him to perform technical passages which call for both
hands. The music builds to a thundering climax, and when it subsides,
a different ostinato figure, in slower tempo, is heard in the orchestra:

Example 25.   Barber, Piano Concerto, Op. 38, Third Movement.

Copyright 1962 by G. Schirmer, Inc. Used by permission.

The piano enters with the theme (Example 25) in widely spaced octaves, giving a ghostly effect to the music, but the solo never plays the
ostinato figure in this second section.

Returning to the original tempo, the main theme with its ostinato
bass reappears. With furious intensity the music builds to a dynamic
peak from which the orchestra again emerges to introduce a third ostinato figure with a new theme in the winds:

Example 26.   Barber, Piano Concerto, Op. 38, Third Movement.

The piano presents its own version of the new idea and a spirited dialogue between orchestra and solo follows. Returning very quietly, the
original ostinato figure sounds unobtrusively and builds gradually but
inevitably to the conclusion of the movement.

In the short time since its composition, the Barber Piano Concerto
has been widely performed in the United States and in Europe. The
immense popularity it has enjoyed will undoubtedly place it securely
in the repertoire. It will be one of the few concertos by American
composers to earn such a position in the company of the great masterworks of the form.

BASIC LISTENING:

RAVEL, Piano Concerto in G major
BARTÓK, Violin Concerto No. 2
PROKOFIEV, Piano Concerto No. 3 in C major
BARBER, Piano Concerto, Op. 38

ADDITIONAL SUGGESTED LISTENING:

BLOCH, Concerto Grosso No. 1 for Strings and Piano
———, *Schelomo* for Cello and Orchestra
RAVEL, Piano Concerto for Left Hand
BARTÓK, Concerto for Orchestra
———, Piano Concerto No. 3
SCHOENBERG, Violin Concerto
BERG, Violin Concerto
STRAVINSKY, Piano Concerto (1924)
———, Capriccio for Piano and Orchestra (1929)
HINDEMITH, Clarinet Concerto (1947)
PROKOFIEV, Violin Concerto No. 2 in G minor

ADDITIONAL READING:

GROUT, DONALD JAY, *A History of Western Music.* New York: W. W.
Norton and Company, Inc., 1960. (Chapter XX: "The Twentieth
Century")

MACHLIS, JOSEPH, *Introduction to Contemporary Music.* New York: W. W. Norton and Company, Inc., 1961.

FOOTNOTES

[1]Nicolas Slonimsky, "Prokofiev," *The Book of Modern Composers,* ed. David Ewen (New York: Alfred A. Knopf, 1942), p. 144.

bibliography

ANDERSON, EMILY, *The Letters of Mozart and His Family*. London: Macmillan and Company, Ltd., 1938.

BLOM, ERIC, *Mozart*. London: J. M. Dent and Sons, 1935.

BOYDEN, DAVID D., *An Introduction to Music*. New York: Alfred A. Knopf, 1966.

BUKOFZER, MANFRED F., *Music in the Baroque Era*. New York: W. W. Norton & Company, Inc., 1947.

EINSTEIN, ALFRED, *Mozart: His Character, His Work*. Translated by Arthur Mendel and Nathan Broder. London: Oxford University Press, 1945.

GEIRINGER, KARL, *Brahms: His Life and Work*. New York: Oxford University Press, 1947.

———, *Haydn*. Second Edition. New York: Doubleday & Co., Inc., 1963. An Anchor Book.

GROUT, DONALD JAY, *A History of Western Music*, shorter edition. New York: W. W. Norton & Company, Inc., 1964.

HOPKINS, ANTHONY, *Talking About Concertos*. Belmont, California: Wadsworth Publishing Company, Inc., 1964.

LANG, PAUL HENRY, *Music in Western Civilization*. New York: W. W. Norton and Company, Inc., 1941.

LEONARD, RICHARD ANTHONY, *A History of Russian Music*. New York: The Macmillan Company, 1957.

MACHLIS, JOSEPH, *Introduction to Contemporary Music*. New York: W. W. Norton & Company, Inc., 1961.

MERSMAN, HANS, *Letters of Wolfgang Amadeus Mozart*. Translated by M. M. Bozman. London: J. M. Dent & Sons, Ltd., 1928.

THAYER, ALEXANDER WHEELOCK, *The Life of Ludwig van Beethoven*. Edited by Henry Edward Krehbiel. New York: G. Schirmer, Inc., 1921. 3 volumes.

TOVEY, DONALD FRANCIS, *Essays in Musical Analysis*. Vol. III, Concertos. London: Oxford University Press, 1936.

TURNER, W. J., *Mozart: The Man and His Works*. New York: Alfred A. Knopf, 1945.

ULRICH, HOMER and PISK, PAUL A., *A History of Music and Musical Style*. New York: Harcourt, Brace & World, Inc., 1963.

VEINUS, ABRAHAM, *The Concerto*. London: Cassell and Company, Ltd., 1948.

index